VILLAGE VOICES

To Narda

VILLAGE VOICES

*Coexistence and Communication
in a Rural Community in Central France*

by Perle Møhl

MUSEUM TUSCULANUM PRESS
UNIVERSITY OF COPENHAGEN
1997

Village Voices
© 1997 by Perle Møhl & Museum Tusculanum Press
Scientific Supervisor: Michael Harbsmeier
Copy editor: Kathleen Fleming
Cover design by Kim Broström
Photos by Perle Møhl
Reproduction of postcards by courtesy of
Ets. M. Roussell, Chateauroux
Printed in Denmark by Narayana Press, Gylling

ISBN 87 7289 344 3

Published with the support from
The Danish Research Council for the Humanities
and Landsdommer V. Gieses Legat

Museum Tusculanum Press
University of Copenhagen
Njalsgade 92
DK-2300 Copenhagen S

CONTENTS

ACKNOWLEDGEMENTS 6

1 INTRODUCTION 7
   1.1 The Line of Inquiry 9
   1.2 "Making Myself at Home": Conflict, Film and Fieldwork 12
   1.3 The Setting 18
   1.4 The Domain of Discourse 24

2 STORIES 29
   2.1 Some Stories 36
   2.2 What the Stories Tell 45
   2.3 Telling Stories: Conditions and Situations 63
   2.4 Stories and Myths 65
   2.5 Conclusion 69

3 EXCHANGING WORDS 71
   3.1 Silence and Discretion 74
   3.2 The Power of Words 92
   3.3 Exchanging: Goods, Deeds, Words 108

4 SPYING 133
   4.1 Countryside Semiotics 135
   4.2 Local Detectives: Seeing, Hearing, Smelling 144
   4.3 Conclusions on Spying 167

5 THE INCONSISTENCIES OF COEXISTENCE 173
   5.1 Being, Doing and Belonging 175
   5.2 Knowledge and Meaning 191
   5.3 Paradoxes of Coexistence 195
   5.4 On Anthropologizing 198

BIBLIOGRAPHY 204

INDEX 209

ACKNOWLEDGEMENTS

I would like to address my warm thoughts and recognition to all those who inspired, encouraged and made possible the development and publication of this book, especially editor Marianne Alenius for her enthusiasm and practical help, Michael Harbsmeier for his wit and his generous advice as scientific supervisor, Kirsten Hastrup for her insight and trust, Jonathan Schwartz for his inspiring comments, Renée Iben for her unwavering support, Kirsten Jørgensen for her perspicacity and valuable observations, and for making the index, Kathleen Fleming for her linguistic assistance which became much more than that, and Vincent for his cooking and his companionship. I also thank the Danish Research Council for the Humanities and Landsdommer V. Giese's Foundation for their financial support.

But above all, I wish to express my infinite gratitude to the people of "La Brumaire," family and friends, who have been working at making meaning out of daily life for years, and who generously taught me some of their wisdom.

1

Introduction

This book is based on approximately eighteen months of fieldwork carried out over several periods from February 1990 to April 1993 in a small village in the Berry region of central France. The village will here be called by the fictive name "La Brumaire," if only to display a tinge of the discretion that I was surrounded by during my stay.

1.1 *The Line of Inquiry*

This work is primarily a study of daily life in a village and its surrounding hamlets as it was lived during the period mentioned above. It is concerned with the forms of communication that arose in that daily life, their modes of expression and of registration. And it is concerned not only with forms, but with content, with the meaning conveyed and created in the process of conveying, through action and through words, spoken or unspoken.

Upon arriving in La Brumaire, I was intrigued by the experience of two apparently significant and contradictory phenomena of communication: that everyone appeared to know absolutely everything about everyone else, and at the same time, that people seemed to be very keen on maintaining silence and discretion and on minding their own business. I was eventually presented with what would turn out to be an unending stream of often quite incredible stories about members of the community, and I was amazed by the amount of detail. I came to discover that talking about others was one of the main social activities, and that every opportunity was taken to discreetly exchange the latest news, reveal knowledge and elaborate on current affairs: at casual meetings on the road, in the post office and local shops, during a work break in the fields, while dropping in for a visit, and of course, at the bistro and in the simmering funeralprocessions. The talking seemed never to stop.

But in that talking and in the gestures surrounding it, very strict principles for exchanging words and information, and the implicit or explicit emphasis on discretion and silence were always being simultaneously expressed. Furthermore, it became clear that silence too was communication, that if it was devoid of sound, it was certainly not devoid of meaning.

Another phenomenon, less remarkable at first but equally important, was people's constant watchfulness over what was going on in and around the village, the ceaseless "reading" of others' activities as though they constituted signs to be juxtaposed and interpreted. I came to liken this to my own preoccupations as a fieldworker, considering the field as composed of signs and deciphering them to find some kind of cultural or social coherence behind. Where I first thought that the difference between the locals and me, the newcomer, was that they knew the "meaning" of the signs, or the "decoding system," and I didn't, I eventually discovered that in all such communication the decoding system itself was being invented. That meaning was not inherent in things and actions but was being continuously deduced from and attached to them. In short, meaning was processual.

This alertness to what others were doing was accompanied by extreme precaution, because one's own activities were naturally subject to the same scrutiny from others. Precaution was expressed not only in silence or very indirect and abbreviated ways of talking, but also in the ways all activities were carried out with immense discretion. The assumption seemed to be that there was always potentially someone spying. And as a matter of fact, when I was going somewhere or just working in the garden, I myself often had the feeling I was not alone and unobserved. As we shall see, this impression increased as the social importance of my actions grew.

The talking and alertness were always centred on other people's *doings* and it occurred to me that somehow "being" had to be linked to "doing" – that the characterization or identification of a person was mainly based on his or her current deeds or doings (which of course included "saying"), and the other way around, that doing was a way of expressing one's being.

The main communicative questions I set out to elucidate were, therefore: how and under what circumstances do knowledge and information circulate; what is the nature of the information; when is there silence; how is action linked to identity, to being; and more generally, what are the conditions of coexistence in La Brumaire? Along with different local categories of group membership and identity, the interlinked and apparently opposed communicative phenomena of knowing, observing, talking, keeping silent, interpreting observations and knowledge, and of exchange became the centre of my investigations.

As will be apparent further on, I was not interested in finding an eventual discrepancy between a "truth" and what people were saying about it. If I was told that Mme. Dupont had an incestuous affair with her brother and as a result her son is mentally deficient, I did not try to ascertain the truth of the statement (how could I, anyway?). I took the same stance I would with myths: the important thing was that it was being said and that it seemed to make sense to the people saying it. My job was to find out something about *how* it made sense, and in a more general way, what "making sense" was about.

My material exposes evident paradoxes, as we have seen. These guided the line of inquiry during the fieldwork and will also be a guideline here. They stirred my curiosity and created an enigma to be pursued. But contrary to the good criminal novel, I didn't solve the enigma and dissolve the paradoxes. I didn't find the killer. So in the following pages, paradoxes will be presented, eventually elucidated, maybe understood, but never quite resolved. For finally, paradoxes can only exist as such – unresolved: that is their very nature. This fact might prove to be one of the "killers" in the end.

1.2 "Making Myself at Home": Conflict, Film and Fieldwork

As Michael Herzfeld says, anthropologists are themselves significant actors in the events they study and therefore have to make sense of the way people make sense of them (1983a). During fieldwork in a village in Rhodes, he was himself seen as a sign of a despised and feared exteriority. He was surrounded by distant/distancing politeness, and because of his reticence to challenge this image, to involve himself in local affairs and "get dirty hands" as he says, this relation never changed throughout his stay. He left the village earlier than scheduled with the impression of having learned much less than what was there to be experienced.

In January 1990, my French husband and I went down to my mother-in-law's house in the Berry, some 350 kilometres south of Paris, to participate in the yearly slaughtering of a pig. During the next two or three days, the former pig – rendered "pork" by a blow to the forehead – would be transformed into roasts, hams, fresh and spiced sausages, black pudding and so forth. I was removing sinews from a shoulder and cutting it into small bits, mixing it with strips of fat, salt and whole pepper to make a spiced sausage, when there was a knock on the kitchen door and Monsieur Tessier stepped in.

A few months earlier, my mother-in-law was approached by a group of neighbours who wanted her to serve as secretary in an association they were forming. They had discovered that a land reallotment process, a *"remembrement,"* had been initiated in the village by the Mayor and a few other farmers, meaning that all the villagers would be expropriated from their land and reassigned new plots whether they liked it or not. The official reason for initiating a reallotment was that the different properties had been dispersed and the size of the fields diminished by subsequent inheritances – because, according to French law, farmlands are equally divided between the heirs – and therefore regrouping was crucial to the intensification of agriculture. In fact, despite the law, primogeniture was quite common, other siblings being more or less willingly bought out of their shares.[1] And otherwise, when conditions

---

1 This form of land inheritance, almost always a source of fraternal dispute, is called the "inegalitarian system" by Segalen and Zonabend, and is a phenomenon which they identify precisely in central and southern France (Segalen & Zonabend 1987: 115).

became too uncomfortable, people managed to exchange fields amongst themselves, finding a reasonable adaptation for the local cow-breeding agriculture.

If some farmlands were scattered it was because certain farmers, the so-called *"affamés de terre"* (land-starved) had bought land just about anywhere. The villagers feared that the reallotment initiators, who were also members of the Commission that was going to preside over the work and evaluate the land, would take all the good land for themselves, leaving only second-rate land and remote fields to the smaller landowners, as had always been the case with other reallotments. Furthermore, land reallotment would mean tearing up a vast number of hedges and groves, and felling the adjoining apple-, pear-, plum- and oak-trees that supplied fruit and firewood. All this to satisfy a small number of farmers and a type of agriculture that, not only in bocage areas like here was showing its economic and ecological limitations, but was also being discouraged by agronomists and by Brussels (Alphandéry et al. 1988).

Nevertheless, the land reallotment was being carried out with funds from Brussels earmarked for underdeveloped regions, and the large amount of money going into just this one land reallotment (around ten million francs for a municipality of 600 inhabitants and about fifty concerned farmers) would certainly create an image of turnover and activity. And of course a lot of entrepreneurs would get work felling trees, tearing down hedges, erecting cement poles and installing barbed wire. As my old geography teacher said, "We all smash some more windows and the GNP goes up." It was very obvious that the principal motivators had nothing to do with raising standards of agriculture, nor with local development in general. (It was yet again, both within Europe and in our relations to the rest of the world, a case of applying the definition of underdevelopment to an area in order to milk the fat cow and drink the cream).

Land reallotments have their own special law whereby the expropriations are justified on account of "collective need," as with highways and railways. A public hearing is announced in the press, and unless more than half of the landowners clearly specify in the so-called *"registre d'enquête"* (inquest registry) that they are against the procedure of land reallotment, it proceeds. In La Brumaire, people did not want a reallotment so they did not go to the meeting. For them, staying home

Villagers showed their opposition towards the land reallotment...

... but the administration won after all.

was a way of showing they were not interested. But for the law, it is the other way around: not clearly expressing oneself against is the same as being for. Two different forms of expression confronted each other, but without communicating. So the procedure was started and from then on, no more objections of any sort could be made.

During his lifetime, Mr. Tessier had managed to build up quite a big, healthy farm through hard work and by buying land or exchanging his own plots with adjacent ones. He was known as a hard worker and a good manager, but was bothered by the fact that his own son would not take over the farm. This embarrassment had been worsened by the recent statement of one of his neighbours, a Commission member: "*Bientôt toutes les terres d'ici jusqu'au croisement seront á moi !*" (Soon, all the land from here to the junction will be mine!), which included all of Tessier's forty hectares. And this was even more exacerbated by the fact that this neighbour, like many in the Commission according to Tessier, belonged to the category *"seigneurs"* or landlords, people who had inherited their land and not worked hard to get it. Such minor conflicts, now aggravated and magnified by the reallotment process, were a common motivation for the people uniting against it.

The villagers understood they had to react, but felt uneasy about facing a mode of discourse they were unfamiliar with – that of the law, and the administrators. They had a tendency to present themselves as bad speakers, as illiterate: "*Nous, on n'sait ni lire ni écrire*" (We don't know how to read or write), which in fact accounts for their enormous caution in handling language, especially when it took as direct and irrevocable a form as written words. So in order to challenge the reallotment and its defenders, they formed an association and asked my mother-in-law to be Secretary, knowing that "she read a lot," had once written a complaint letter to the Mayor on behalf of a neighbour, and was, like them, against the land reallotment for both social and ecological reasons. She accepted their request.

So now M. Tessier had come by to discuss the next steps to be taken. They were gathering signatures in the municipality and had already obtained nearly 300 (which represented about 70-80% of the landowners).

Engaged in our sausage-making, we sensed that something important was at stake for these people, more than just a few acres of land.

First of all, that land – often passed down for generations and named after the family, sometimes bought through years of work and savings – was more than just a working tool. It was their entire social justification, it was them. Moreover, even if these properties were not big farms, they were, despite the growing and now almost total influence of the authorities in all agricultural and rural matters, what provided their owners' self-sufficiency and independence. That was, they thought, one of the unassailable rights gained by the Revolution. And for those who were retired or just owned a little piece of land, that land was their anchorage in the local space. Arguments that looked at first like, and were treated as, old-fashioned sentimentalism and protectionism up against modern collective reason, were in fact very fundamental expressions of what it meant to be someone from somewhere and take important decisions in one's life. It was a struggle about power and democracy, about the dwindling diversity and rootedness of rural France – rootedness and diversity that normally keep silent, but which must talk when their existence is at stake.

We realized that if there were ever an opportunity to witness those otherwise-so-silent-and-discreet people express the essentials of their communal life, this was it. So we asked if we could follow and participate in the events with our camera and microphone. The members of the association, not accustomed to prying cameras but knowing they were already engaged in a reign of discourse so completely different from their ordinary one, accepted. They hoped the camera would be a useful tool in witnessing injustices and conveying their sentiments.

We started shooting on February 15, 1990, and finished in the summer of 1993. As the film shows, the conflict was eventually lost and the bulldozers moved in, although at times – like when the town hall displayed the project maps and was occupied by about a hundred people, and the Mayor was verbally attacked in front of the press – it seemed as if the battle might be won. But somehow the stakes were too high (since accomplishing this first reallotment in the region, a whole series of others has been initiated), and the efforts and determination of the villagers too weak. For a moment, they thought perhaps they did have an influence on the important matters of their lives after all, until finally they were forced to acknowledge they had been right in thinking they did not. In my opinion, they faced an agricultural crisis no one had a solution to, they least of all, and were afraid of hindering the only alternative, although obviously a bad one, and of being held responsible for the continual deterioration of the local situation. Letting go, giving up, they ended up being the ones both wronged and proved right in the first place.

Making a film and, actually, just being there, involved me in the process, for one could hardly stand by as a neutral observer and not be outraged by the irrationality of the affair and the abuses of power. On a practical level, apart from filming, I undertook some of the administrative work that could conveniently be done on a computer, and also tried to get an idea of the legal implications by reading the relevant laws. The reallotment was so obviously unjust, so obviously non-social and non-ecological, it played on people's fear and obedience, and they felt helpless. So going back to the beginning and to Herzfeld, who kept his hands clean and therefore never came to know, the position I had as a fieldworker was clearly the opposite: I was the relative of a local person, heavily engaged in a local conflict, active in the work of the Association and a chronicler of the process, and that was how I was seen by the locals: not as a neutral inquirer (that is never the case anyway), but as a highly involved, dirty-handed interlocutor. Had I not made a film, had I not taken a stance, had I not been related to someone who was herself involved, I would never have had a position within the local social space and there would have been no reason for them to address me with anything other than polite trivialities.

1.3 The Setting

I have chosen to limit my investigations to the municipality of La Brumaire. Ethnographically speaking this is a rather arbitrary unit, for nothing else in local categories and formations follows the administrative municipal border. But as a unit, it is also simply a practical one. Furthermore, it coincides with the limits of the land reallotment, and as we have seen, within this otherwise arbitrary space I had a position, i.e., "dirty hands." In the specific context of the reallotment, the otherwise hollow administrative category of "municipality" became dense and invested with meaning (cf. Ardener 1972b). When in the following account I refer to "Brumairians," this should hence be understood as an analytical construct referring to a probability, and not as an empirical entity.

Of course, the flow and exchange of knowledge and stories had no physical or administrative borders, but were ordered around each individual, forming an uneven sphere that followed the extent of that individual's social horizon. The analysis therefore inevitably includes material and stories from outside municipal borders, but only insofar as they have a basis in and a meaning for the village inhabitants. Otherwise, these stories would not have been told and I would not have heard them. Hence, my field of investigation is amorphous and mushroom-like, taking root in La Brumaire, yet casting its shadow somewhat beyond the municipal borders.

La Brumaire is a relatively small municipality of approximately 600 inhabitants, situated in the Boischaut Sud of the Berry region in central France. Long and narrow, it lies in the northern spurs of the Massif Central at an altitude of about 300 metres. The landscape is hilly, green and lush, abundant with forests and thickets, traversed by numerous brooks. An intricate system of dense hedges, delineating a multitude of small fields of various colours, gives the impression of a chessboard from a distance, the typical *"bocage"* landscape. The topsoil is thin, and here and there, the rocky ground lies bare. So despite the lushness, the green slopes are more adequate as pastures than for cultivation, and raising limousine cattle and some sheep constitutes the main agricultural activity. Some fields are cultivated, usually providing enough fodder for the livestock but hardly any surplus for selling.

Small-scale agriculture

The Bocage landscape

Apart from the main village, *"le bourg,"* inhabited by about one-fifth of the population, the municipality is composed of forty-one hamlets with between one and twelve or fifteen inhabitants residing in each. Over the last century, the area has witnessed a considerable decrease in population, from around 1500 inhabitants in 1905 to the 600 of today, with a marked fall in the period from 1968 to 1975. The first year after the census of 1990, we further counted six burials and two births. A large part of the population comprises retired peasants and artisans (about 30 % in 1982), and many of the active farmers are in their forties and fifties, and unmarried. Only one-fifth of the households counted children under the age of seventeen in 1982. So the demographic situation is not improving, and a very perceptible "end-of-the-world" ambience is prevailing. If the present agricultural crisis doesn't get the better of the village, the lack of young inhabitants certainly will.

La Brumaire, and the Boischaut Sud more generally, are rather poor in terms of economic development and production, and the department figures among the poorest of the country. There is practically no industry, and infrastructures are hardly developed. If the considerable economic differences between the intensively cultivated wheat plains in the north of the department and the extensive farming and breeding in the south were taken into account, the Boischaut Sud would register even further down the scale. These are of course statistical and administrative figures calculated from a centralized, economist's perspective, where investments and expenses, as we have seen with the land reallotment, may raise economic turnover without raising the standard of living. And these figures do not necessarily reflect local conditions.

As a matter of fact, wealth is apparently measured in La Brumaire less in terms of actual income and "turnover" than in terms of what one has – land, machines, cattle, allies – and what one has to give – like eggs, vegetables and a helping hand. A large majority of the inhabitants depend directly upon or supplement their income with agriculture. Everyone has an extensive vegetable garden, and relatively low incomes are thus complemented by vegetables, eggs, milk, some meat, wood for heating and so on. So even if many locals, and certainly the farmers, officially earn far less than the minimum wage (*le S.M.I.C.*), they survive through what comes close to a local self-sufficiency, exhibited in and enforced by the healthy exchange of goods and deeds that still takes place. The level of self-sufficiency is of course nowhere near what it was only twenty or thirty years ago when very few items were purchased from tradesmen, especially when it came to wooden utensils and victuals. People have become dependent on industrially made machines, tools, and even some food, and thus on cash incomes. But still, an alternative internal economy based on local self-sufficiency seems to subsist alongside the official one, and to defy any impression of poverty.

On a comparative scale, economic differences within the community are relatively small, with the exception of a few villagers who have jobs outside the village and seem to be slightly better off than farmers and local craftsmen. Among farmers, differences prevail as to the number of cattle and the extent of land exploited, but this does not necessarily reflect a difference in wealth. Farmers that seem more prosperous, both to the outsider and in terms of economic figures, are often burdened by heavy mortgages on their property and livestock and sometimes live on the verge of bankruptcy, whereas apparently smaller farmers often profit from having many fewer expenses and no mortgage. Not only does this situation make actual incomes somewhat level, but it further relativizes differences because local conceptions of wealth operate with a distinction between what one owns and what one disposes of through loans. Furthermore, many big farmers have very little land of their own and depend on renting fields from others, whereas some smaller farmers own all their land. In both cases, not depending on bank loans and owning one's land, the primary parameter of wealth is autonomy.

Generally speaking, wealth, property and income are private matters that one never boasts about or even reveals to others, as we shall see. It is therefore quite difficult to estimate the actual situation. But since this study is not concerned with analyzing economics as a separate sphere isolated from the discursive field, wealth and economics shall only interest us as special topics to the extent, and in the ways, that they are articulated in definitions of the self and others, along with a multitude of other categories and criteria. And here, it shall be seen, the chief interest is not in individual, quantitative wealth, but in the balance of exchange: having is being able to give, and thus withhold; it is a potential. Wealth is a qualitative category, measured in action. The local discrimination between innate and acquired property, between those who inherited and those who worked for what they have, may to some extent be seen as an exception to this rule. At the same time this discrimination confirms the rule exactly by distinguishing a process (wealth through work) from something given, more instantaneous (wealth through inheritance).

As for the relationship between life in the village and in the outside world, the impression of isolation and introversion that one has upon arriving in La Brumaire is soon confirmed in both explicit remarks and in everyday communication patterns in general, as shall be seen later. Most people have television, many read the local newspaper, *La Nouvelle République,* and are concerned with what goes on outside their immediate social environment. But in talking, even if such subjects are touched upon, primary attention is clearly given to events arising in the community and to the evolution of internal affairs. What goes on outside the social sphere of individuals apparently has less impact on their ongoing definition of themselves and others. This is not to say that life in La Brumaire evolves in isolation from the motions of the world in general: such an insular view would be unrealistic and false. But when it comes to social and individual identities, relations between the local and the outside world are most commonly articulated in terms of inequality, non-exchange, non-dialogue, distance. Again, the internal articulation of the world interests us here, not phenomena that are determined independently of local communication.

Le Berry, Les Patois
La Brumaire is situated in Le Berry, which more or less coincides with the two departments, Indre and Cher, as they were delimited during the French Revolution (Denizet et al. 1982). Le Berry is not an administrative but rather a cultural and linguistic entity, defined as such mainly by folklorists (Bernard 1982; Boncoeur 1983; de La Salle 1900, 1902; Rochet-Lucas 1980). But a quick look at the area's history characterizes it more as a scene of constant battle between varying peoples, counties and fiefdoms than as a unified cultural space.

If there were any historical constant here it would be in the name itself, whereas the areas actually referred to by that name change, and their appropriation by various warring factions shifts. From the Celtic *"civitas bituricum,"* a much broader expanse than the actual Berry, through *"Le Comté de Bourges"* around the year 500, to the independent *"Comté de Berry"* in the Middle Ages, the area has been fought over, but mainly *on*, by Romans versus Celts, Visigoths versus Franks, the English of Aquitaine against the Capetian kingdom around Paris in the 12th century, and in between, by a variety of smaller combatting groups and duchies. In these conflicts, through marriages and power transfers, Le Berry or parts of it have often changed sides, now allied to the north, now to the south. Like most political units without natural borders, the territory of Le Berry has varied in shape and size, shedding some estates, taking in others through war, marriage, inheritance. During the Hundred Year War against the English in the 14th and 15th century, chaos virtually reigned, counties fighting counties, estates fighting estates (Denizet et al. 1982: 15-38).

Traces of this tumultuous history are still present in the landscape with its many fortified castles in ruins. Thus, from the early Middle Ages to the Revolution, the lands that today constitute the municipality of La Brumaire, located at the outskirts of Le Berry, have belonged to different estates, sometimes connected to Le Berry, sometimes to the County of La Marche in the south.

Today, the village is still marked by divided allegiances, for people in the southern part of the municipality tend to turn southward to the geographically closer village across the county (and regional) border. Many went to school there, do their shopping there, and choose to get married and buried there. They also tend to read the newspaper from the area south of them. And as we shall see later, the more practical aspects of the north-south cleavage are enforced by a conscious, almost deliberate language cleavage that cuts the long municipality in two: in the south a local dialect or *patois* is spoken which people identify as *"marchois"* (from La Marche), as opposed to the *"berrichon"* spoken in the north of the municipality. Language is, especially in France perhaps, a strong instrument in identifying oneself and others, and in this specific case it is skilfully used to play on a whole set of other distinctions separating the north of France from the south, *l'Occitanie*. Nevertheless, it is my impression that the *berrichon* of the north and the *marchois* of the south are both transitional forms rather than pure dialects, and that from a broader perspective, they have more in common than at variance. The use of categories of *patois* will be discussed later.

1.4 The Domain of Discourse

The present work inscribes itself within a series of related anthropological studies of communities (or "virtual communities") and their forms of social interpretation and identity creation. What these studies have in common is that they are centred on discourse, they approach social phenomena as signs, they emphasize individual interpreters and the variety of interpretations, and they show a general predilection for the creative and negotiable qualities of social life. Furthermore, most of them deal explicitly with the role of the interpreting anthropologist.

Let me first mention the writings of Jeanne Favret-Saada on sorcery in the Norman Bocage of northwest France (1971, 1977, 1986, 1987, 1989; Favret-Saada & Contreras 1981). In this extensive work, she identifies sorcery as the accusation and treatment of bewitchment – that is, as the discourse *about* sorcerers and spells rather than the actual practice of casting spells. She thus appreciates the social scenery through, or rather in, the discourses about it. The notion of "virtual communities" refers particularly to her descriptions of sorcery because, as we shall see later (Chapter 3.2), the "community" exists only on the level of discourse, as a group of individuals who are "taken" (*prise*), and not on a general societal level. Sorcery is not something one is brought up with, but a discursive domain one may enter if and when one is identified by someone already inside the discursive sphere as having been exposed to sorcery and thus being "*prise.*" This is also significant for her own approach and access to the sphere.

The discourses of sorcery comprise only a small and specific part of the much larger field of talking about others and identifying oneself in relation to them. Nevertheless, the discourses of sorcery reflect an idea of counterbalance that reoccurs in the general themes of coexistence and reciprocal influence encountered in La Brumaire.

Another related study is that of Michael Herzfeld, who describes the formation of identity among shepherds in a small village in Crete (1985). His was particularly interested in the ways individuals become who they are through skilfully describing what they have achieved, a discursive mode he identifies as "poetics." He focuses on individuals (males), and how they achieve being ("a man"), both by doing ("stealing") and by talking ("about stealing"). As Herzfeld sees it, Cretans operate in and make meaning out of daily life through their own, locally developed semiotic theories, or what they call "simasia." The concept of simasia is not limited to ideas and words, but also comprises action; meaning is thus identified as poetic or performative rather than simply linguistic (ibid.: xiv). Without clearly defining the relationship to semiotic theory in general, Herzfeld hence develops the concept of ethnosemiotics.

In another study, he discusses the uses of categories in the production and negotiation of one's own and others' identities, for example Rhodesian villagers' skilled use of different languages or "diglossia," to distance themselves from others (1983a). Finally, he also focuses on interactions of and with the fieldworker, and the negotiation of his role (1981b, 1983a, 1983b, 1985).

A third and related study is Anne Knudsen's analysis of Corsican vendettas (1989a). Her study has historical and theoretical implications of its own, but it joins the other studies in its concern with the continuous production of honour and identity among individuals, and the way people negotiate their solidarity and credibility through interaction. She first identifies a kinship system that does not define distinct groups, very similar to the conditions I observed. She then determines that belonging to specific groups is revealed in the formation of "*ad hoc* solidarity" groups. And finally, she identifies vendettas as the most powerful mechanism for expressing solidarity and belonging through significant actions and choices – actions and choices that moreover put life in utmost danger. Her theoretical approach is semiotic: actions are signs, they produce and convey meaning, and thus they can be included within a discursive mode of identity production.

One thing these diverse studies have in common with my study is a focus on discourse; they all consider discourse an autonomous sphere that cannot be reduced to other societal spheres. On the contrary, other aspects of society can only be conceived of through discourse. Ultimately, as it shall be argued, they do not even exist as societal outside discourse.

Actions are considered as belonging to the domain of discourse in the sense that they may produce and convey meaning, that they are signs. The domain of discourse is thus broader than the strictly linguistic or verbal field.

Furthermore, like these studies, the present work sets the interpreting individual at the centre of the analysis. This opens the study up to variation and diversity in the production of meaning, on the level of both articulation and interpretation ("writing" and "reading").

As for the "units" of study, Knudsen deals with Corsicans, inhabitants of a well defined unity enclosed by water, and Herzfeld with Glendiots in an enclosed area defined by village limits, whereas both Favret-Saada and I take *discourse* as our point of departure, and then define our units from there. There is no community, no social, outside discourse. Whereas for Favret-Saada's study we can actually talk about a "virtual community," the Brumaire study operates with a slightly more "palpable" unit, which nevertheless must be redefined at every moment and for each individual, reflecting the extent of their social acquaintances and knowledge (cf. Chapters 1.3 + 2.2).

Finally, these studies are all explicitly concerned with the position of the anthropologist and his or her access to knowledge. Along the lines of Edwin Ardener, with whom the anthropologists mentioned here also have many other themes in common, it follows from the positions outlined above that the anthropologist is only one among many interpreting and analyzing subjects.

Taking one's departure from discourse and making it the field of inquiry has certain implications. For one, societal phenomena are at issue here only insofar as, and in the ways that, they are present in discourse. This means that apart from the short introductory view of the setting given above, I will make no attempt to include parameters that could be said to be established independently of internal conceptions. Furthermore, there will be no attempt to see discourses in the light of such phenomena, to reveal eventual discrepancies between local interpretations and phenomena defined by external criteria, or even to operate with a truth outside what people say and relate. As previously mentioned, I am not trying to say something factual about, for example, rates of incest, but to examine the ways such supposed acts are dealt with and interpreted in, or perhaps omitted from, the stories told.

So using discourse as a point of departure implies that operating with standard, external categories such as economics, gender or age is pointless if they seem to have no local significance. This study therefore makes no distinction between the respective ways men and women go about talking, nor between possible differences in the subjects discussed. Obviously this does not mean that people in La Brumaire make no distinctions between men and women, but that these differences did not seem decisive to either discursive modes or content. The same could be said of age differences, the only exception being very young children, who had not yet learned the art of discretion. As for economic differences, I have already mentioned that wealth has little to do with quantitative figures, but is rather articulated through exchange, an idea I will develop later. The main thing is, such differences certainly do not impinge upon discursive modes. This is as true for economic difference as for gender and age difference: everyone is equally subject to being talked about, thereby equally attributed social existence, and everyone is equally subject to talking. The same can be said for most other external categories of distinction. Some matters are certainly more interesting, more defining, than others, but broaching this discussion here would be premature.

Finally, as we shall see, using discourse and process as points of departure enhances the dimension of inconstancy. So if Brumairians themselves sometimes operate with what one could identify as "internal objective structures" or categories, even these categories have no stable content but are constantly being redefined through discourse.

As a rule, I will make no attempt to operate with objective structures with which local discourse and society might be compared and measured. On the contrary, if such structures exist, not only can they only be analyzed through discourse, but ultimately, they do not exist outside discourse. For discourse in the broad sense of the term not only reflects society, it creates and encompasses society; it is society.

2

Stories

While dealing with the land reallotment and trying to estimate the number of landowners who might reject expropriation, I was often told an informal story or two to help me understand a certain person's motivations for being either for or against the procedure of reallotment. This was an indication that such choices were motivated more often by pre-existing alliances and conflicts than by the actual issues and material interests.

It occurred to me that in telling these stories, my interlocutors were sketching what one might call the "social landscape." The stories often established family connections, friendships, and alliances between people and accounted for conflicts, some dating back to distant generations and to matters other than land. Knowing the landscape and the relationships between people today would make their choices more predictable for me, and would also prevent me from committing tactical mistakes like buying my bread in the wrong shop or addressing someone I ought not to do. It became obvious that in order to move around easily in the social landscape of the village, one had to know which inhabitants not to trip over, as it were. Just as myths reveal the world, these stories revealed and defined the current state of affairs in the village as interpreted by the particular narrators.

It eventually occurred to me that the stories were more than just verbal reflections of the society that nourished them. In a society where words are so well guarded, what is the point of saying in words what is there to be observed directly with the eyes? The stories seemed to detach themselves from the social, and gain some kind of independence that had its own influence upon the social. There was no simple one-to-one relation between narrative and social, discernible by rules of deduction or causality. In that respect, my *raconteurs* were not only describing the social landscape, they were also constructing it.

Sometimes the stories were banal, but most of the time they were quite amazing. From accounts of everyday incidents like drinking, fighting, theft and conflict between neighbours or relatives, they also included tales of madness, murder, suicide, infanticide, incest, pyromania, and fatal accidents, sometimes with vague allusions to sorcery. The incredible thing was that not only were these things supposedly going on around us, but furthermore, that they were being exposed with such apparent ease and acceptance. I was amazed by the amount of detail and the kinds of things people noticed and commented on, attached importance to and thus knew about each other's private lives, and by the fact that this knowledge apparently never led to official persecutions or local, internal condemnations. People continued associating with each other, working together, greeting one another on the street, buying their groceries, occasionally avoiding but never overtly condemning individuals.

Another striking thing was the extent of the story-telling. It became clear that talking about others was the most important communicative activity of social life, constituting what could almost be considered the "oral tradition" of the community. Although talking was subject to very strong limitations (as we shall see), it seemed never to stop. Every opportunity was taken to exchange the latest news, follow up on a story, speculate on the developments of a recent event. It was this peculiar contradiction between silence/secrecy and candid talking that caught my attention: if story-telling defied taboos, it had to be significant — more than just idle chatter.

It also became clear that the stories — what people said about each other and what they called special attention to — could be invaluable sources of knowledge, not so much about what the characters were actually doing, but as an insight into "village knowledge" and internal values and evaluations. I chose to take the stories seriously and treat them as an entry into the continual internal definition and redefinition of oneself and others.

When I use the word "stories" to characterize talking about others, it is partly to shed the common (and scientific) negative connotations of words like "gossip" and "rumours." It is also because information was often presented this way: as whole narratives with a beginning, a climax and an end. Sometimes there were just faint allusions to a story, sometimes whole stories created on the spot by consecutive comments and interjections from various participants in the conversation. Sometimes past events were conveyed in accounts that were almost mythical in nature, as we shall see. The distinction to be made between full-fledged stories and mere chatter is vague. Rather than a clear dichotomy, it would be more useful to think of a progressive line between two relative points, a question of form rather than content. In Chapter 2.1 the distinction is not marked, and everything from sporadic remarks to complete stories is taken into account.

Before undertaking the analysis of the stories, I would like to critique several anthropological theories of gossip and rumour, and explain why for the time being I avoid using these terms, so commonly applied to village talk.

In his discussion of the social function of what he chose to call "gossip," Max Gluckman's greatest merit was to take it seriously as something more than a trivial pastime occupation (1963, 1968). But his defence of gossip dealt more with its form than its content. In itself, gossip could not lead to information about other parts of society and was, as a result, perceived and studied as an isolated phenomenon. The primary interest of gossip lay in its *function* as a community delimiter (literally), excluding outsiders from participating in the act and pointing to them as "outsiders," as opposed to the participating "insiders" (Gluckman 1963: 308-9). According to this argument, content was important only in that outsiders did not "have" it and therefore could not engage in gossiping. Inversely, according to the same logic, members of the group were forced to gossip to affirm their membership (ibid.: 313). Content was significant to Gluckman only when it stipulated and enforced rules by talking of transgressions – like the function of punishing criminals (ibid.: 315) – thereby conforming the moral values of the group, and again, serving as a useful "cultural technique" for maintaining group unity. But if the unit of analysis is the act of gossiping itself, the logic of the argument would require that the person in question actually heard the gossip (which was rarely the case), in the same way he or she would suffer directly from imprisonment. Secondly, as we shall see, talking about others does not necessarily imply moral condemnation, although this is not evident if the stories are analyzed by themselves, as they are by Gluckman, and not seen over the background of day-to-day life. Finally, the group-unity argument requires that gossipers consider themselves as belonging to one and the same group, which, at least when it comes to La Brumaire, is not at all the case. The picture is much more complex.

Another more general criticism of Gluckman's approach is that according to him, gossip consists only of negative slander and therefore needs no further analysis because it is devoid of meaning on any level other than that of function. What people are actually saying is irrelevant, as though they were not conveying meaning.

Most of those who responded to Gluckman's exposés (e.g., Abrahams 1970; Handelman 1973; Kapferer,B. 1975; Lancaster 1974; Paine 1967, 1968) did not deviate substantially from his functionalist line, although some turned the focus from group solidarity to individual interest and information-management in a kind of transactional functionalism. In his examination of social encounters, Handelman sought "to show that whether the transmission of gossip is successfully accomplished... with greater or less difficulty depends at least in part on the kinds of encounters within which such attempts at information transmission are made" (Handelman 1973: 210) – which makes me think more of artificial insemination than chatting human beings. In a very meticulous German study on gossip, *"Klatsch,"* Bergmann remarks that the fault of such analysis lies in isolating the social elements – morality, group unity and information management – on functionalist grounds. He notes that the dynamic and character of *"Klatsch"* arise precisely from the fact that all these elements coexist, play with, contrast with and neutralize one another (Bergmann 1987: 205).

One thing all these contributors have in common is that they omit studying the information conveyed by gossip. They are apparently ill-at-ease with this unhealthy and obviously non-social activity, unfortunately so cherished by the people they study. This inclines these researchers to justify gossip on precisely socio-functional grounds, and to let form rule out content. Taking gossip seriously, let alone enjoying it, seems to be out of their range.

This tendency is even more manifest in a series of French sociological investigations that attempted to understand the mechanisms of rumours and their modes of diffusion, mainly with the quite exorbitant aim of stopping them because of their mass-suggestive (and often commercially destructive) effects. In an analysis of the so-called *"rumeur d'Orléans"* in the late sixties, Morin actually talks about three stages in the development of rumours – incubation, propagation and metastasis – and about residue and germs (Morin 1969: 23-37), while other researchers just talk about an "infectious disease" (*maladie contageuse*), as J.-N. Kapferer notes (1990: 20). The contributors all agree in their definition of rumours as having no basis in reality, characterized only by virtue of their falseness (ibid.: 19-23).

The question of truth or falsity is not very interesting and it certainly doesn't bring us any closer to understanding the phenomena. As Hastrup notes, the fact that the truth cannot be verified does not make it a lie (Hastrup 1986: 13). In my opinion, this holds true for both ethnographers' and other people's stories and statements. But the true/false question has nevertheless been widely disseminated when it comes to areas of culture that could not be directly perceived by the researcher (and were not therefore verifiable), and especially to everyday talk, which is in fact rarely identified as "culture." The extreme of this implication for scientific approaches would be that what people go around saying about each other is of no semantic value. As we shall see, my point of departure is quite different.

Once, after telling the story of a woman who had all her children with her own brother, I was asked by a fellow anthropologist how I could be sure that it was true. The answer was simple: I couldn't. How could I, by asking her? But actually, my main objection is of another order: whether people are relating certified facts or not is quite irrelevant for my specific purpose. The value of such a story is not as a factual statement about incest in the community. The interest, the reality of the story is that it is being told and therefore it, and the telling of it, makes sense, is significant to the people telling, listening, remembering and repeating it – or omitting it. On the basis of this, I will undertake the further analysis of the stories.

2.1 Some Stories

A number of stories follow, some of them in several versions. The aim is to give insight into the intimacy of village knowledge about neighbours, to illustrate the nature of the stories, and to lay the groundwork for a preliminary analysis of both content and context on various levels. The stories here were chosen mainly as good examples, but of course some are more significant than others. A few are also included for their entertainment value.

I never recorded dialogue, nor did I take notes in front of people. I was not conducting interviews, I was taking part in casual conversation, and any "investigative artifice" would have destroyed the atmosphere and stopped the talking, even if people knew very well I was studying communication. The wording of the stories is thus based on notes taken after encounters, and I relied on my memory and my own sense of significance, in the same way that other people remember, interpret and retell stories. The selection is based on a sense of the stories' social significance and typicality, both in form and content. Stories are reproduced here in English with casual reference to idiomatic French expressions. Titles are applied by me for convenience. As elsewhere in the text, the names are fictive.

(1) The Child in the Dunghill

Version A:
Don't tell anyone this (*"Il faut pas l'dire"*): The Dubois girl shoved a dead baby into the dunghill. It started smelling. The dunghill was in the courtyard just next to the street where everyone passed by. Her father was a grocer, and you had to pass right by the dunghill to do your shopping. And it smelled bad. It smelled evil (*"Ça sentait mauvais. Ça sentait le mal"*). But she's a hard-working girl!

Finally, because of the smell, they found it. Nothing happened to her though; they knew someone, a policeman. The next day she went to church! I saw her there myself. But don't tell anyone, eh... *M'il faut pas l'dire, hein...*

Version B:
Did you know? They threw a baby in the dunghill after killing it. The daughter who no longer lives there. Seems it was a bit deformed (crooked, *"de travers"*), so they strangled it or I don't know what, and they threw it in the dunghill.

Version C:
The B's: [1]
> We don't know about those things, it wasn't here... Here, a girl, in the house up there, after...

P: Oh, the Dubois girl, Pelletier's daughter?
B's: Yes. She knows things better than us! Well, it appears (*"il paraît que"*) that she put a baby in some ashes. So it wouldn't smell bad.
P: Yes, like hams...
B's: Well, hams, that's to preserve them... A baby, it... well, it's not preserved, it disappears. Hams are salted... She put it in a sack with ashes and hid it in the chimney.
P: And someone found it?
B's: Well, yes...
P: Was she taken to court?
B's: Well, she was, but since the priest defended her... She was on good terms with him and he defended her, so they let her go. Nothing happened to her.
P: Did someone turn her in?
B's: Well, no... Everyone saw she was pregnant, and afterwards, she wasn't any more. Everyone saw it, eh.

Version D ("Silent" Version):
A: When I came back here, it was hard to get work. So after a while I started working for the Pelletier's. That was fine, I worked there for six months, they were good people.
P: But they say... (*"on dit que"*)
A: Oh, people say just about anything! Anything at all. They should just worry about their own affairs, that's all. The Pelletier's are good people and that's that!

---

1 "B's" stands for a couple, speaking in turn, "P" for myself.

(2) The Thieving Family
My, they were thieves. They stole apples in people's gardens at night. The husband too, although he was from an honest family. And she stole milk. One night we heard noises from the stable – we slept just above – and I went down to see. I thought something was wrong with the cow. And there she was, milking our cow! And she just said: "Would you like some too?" Can you imagine? Only she could think of a thing like that. Oh, my, did they steal! ... We were more ashamed for them than they were! My husband always said that he was more ashamed than they were!

(3) The Young Girl in the Storm "au Gâtinet"
C: You know what happened? A young couple was walking home from the fields, crossing the *Gâtinet*. The girl's younger sister was walking behind them. It was raining and the couple was carrying an umbrella. Suddenly lightning struck the umbrella and the young girl dropped dead. Nothing happened to the other two.
   The story is repeated to a second person:
D: Oh, you know what happened? A young girl died up on the *Gâtinet* when...
Thérèse (an old woman):
   Yes, yes, I know. She was supposed to be my godmother. I was being baptized the next morning. The dress was lying ready on the bed, and my mother very quickly had to find another girl who could fit it.

(4) The Bastard Goes to his Father's Wedding
Version A: They were supposed to get married, the Dumas girl and young Chavenaud. She was having his child. But then he married another girl whom he had also got pregnant. The Dumas girl and her father showed up in church the day of his wedding, and the girl had her newborn baby in her arms.

Version B: No, he didn't acknowledge it as his, I don't think. The kid wasn't called Chavenaud. Chavenaud is my cousin, by the way.

(5) The Window
Her daughter was not quite normal; a bit deformed (crooked, *"de travers"*), you know. Then one day – she was already quite old – she fell from the window upstairs and was killed... They say she didn't fall all by herself...

(6) The Brigand Sisters
Version A:
E: Everything has changed here, all the old-timers (*"les anciens"*) are gone.
P: Well, there's still Aubourg, and the Delaveau's. Are they related?
E: Yes, they're cousins. Well... There was Robert Aubourg's father and Gaston Delaveau's father; both married Brigand girls – two sisters – and were neighbours. The two farms came from the Brigand family. (*"Les deux domaines étaient de souche Brigand."*) And both couples had children. But then Aubourg was killed, kicked in the head by a horse at the market at La Châtre. What a disaster, he wasn't very old. I remember, I was fourteen years old. So Clémence found herself widowed, alone with her children and the farm.
P: Yes, but her sister lived next door, didn't she? She could have helped her...
E: Well, yes, but she died too.
P: Oh, yeah?
E: Yes! One year later, to the day (*"un ans après, jour pour jour"*). I remember, in the morning she passed by with her bucket, she was going to her garden, and the very same evening she was dead. It wasn't normal. She wasn't ill, and then she dropped dead just like that. And I assure you, she died a year after Aubourg, on the exact same date. That wasn't normal...
P: No, it does seem a bit strange, actually...
E: So Aubourg's grandfather, Gaston's father, was a widower too. And they decided to put the properties together, that's what they said. And they got married. And there were more children from the second marriage (*"le deuxième lit"*), two of them. Alfred and his sister there. Delaveau already had three children from the first marriage (*"le premier lit"*), Gaston and two girls.

P: So Gaston and his sisters lived with their aunt, their cousins and their half-brother and half-sister?
E: No, she didn't take care of them, only her own children. The others went to live with an aunt on their father's side.
P: It can't have been simple with the inheritance.
E: Oh, no! It wasn't simple. And you see, now, with the land reallotment, they're all on their own side.

Version B:
P: Gaston's mother was a Brigand, wasn't she?
F: Yes, and she was the sister of Aubourg's mother. But she died very young; Gaston, my husband, was only four years old. There were three children, he was the eldest. The smallest was only one or two. They say she died from mixing milk and blood.
P: What do you mean by that?
F: Well, when she was breast-feeding Lucienne...

(7) The Jacket
You know what happened? Faugère from Grabant was going home from the field and had put his jacket behind him on the tractor. Grosrichard was behind him on the road for a while. When Faugère got home, he realized he lost his jacket along the way. He went back to look for it, taking the same route, no jacket! So he went to see Grosrichard to ask him if he might have picked it up for him. Grosrichard says: "No, no, I didn't see anything" (*"je n'ai rien vu"*). But when Faugère gets up to leave, what does he see behind a chair? His jacket. He said nothing, of course. But now everyone knows.

(8) Riolet and the Cows
P: Do you know of anyone who has special faculties (*"des dons spéciaux"*) around here, who knows how to cast spells (*"qui savent jeter des sorts"*)?
E: Not around here. They believe in that elsewhere, but that's supertis... superstition. Just because a calf dies doesn't mean it's a spell. Or because someone has a car accident. Some people have luck, others don't. That's all.
    ...

P: I read in a book about a man who gets accused of being a sorcerer just because he happens to have a problem with his moped while passing in front of someone's house. The unwitcher said the sorcerer would be the first one to ask a favour, and it happened to be...
E: Oh, yes. Here... my parents had a good cow, but when I left for the war, she had a calf and after that, there was no way to milk her, you couldn't get close anymore. The calf could, but they sold it young, as they did in those days. So the old Riolet, Marcelle's father, came by, and he said: "Looks like a nice cow, would you sell it?" They said she was ornery (*"qu'elle était ch'ti'"*), not all that nice, but he still wanted to buy it. And already the next morning he was milking her out in the open field, without even tying her up!
P: So he was gifted?
E: Well, it's not to say that.. but... Well, some years later, he sold a good cow to my cousin, Marie from Grabant. I saw it calve when I was working for him, it was a fine cow, gave lots of milk. But the moment it arrived in my cousins yard, it went dry (*"elle s'est tarie"*). Not a single drop left... You almost have to believe it... He cast a spell on it and sold it.
P: Yes...
E: There's also the change of surroundings. That does something too. Maybe the cow felt better at his place. Maybe he had a way (*"qu'il savait y faire"*) with animals.

(9) Labaye's Eye
Version A:
P: Who's Arthème Labaye? A relative of Labaye?
G: Yes, but they're no longer on speaking terms (*"ils se causent plus"*). It's his father... Didn't you see Labaye's eye? They were fighting about some hay and his father shot at him.
P: Oh, yeah? Recently?
G: Four years ago. They'd been quarrelling because Labaye wanted to take some hay and his father wouldn't let him. So he left and came back in the evening to take it anyway. And his father came out with his shotgun and fired at him, and hit him in the eye. The bullet hit right here. He could have killed him.
P: Didn't the police come?

G: Well, yes, they came. But he never lodged a complaint, so... But they no longer talk.

Version B:
P: It seems like old Labaye is rather violent.
H: Well, not really. But he was afraid of his son, that's why he fired. His son came to claim some hay and they started quarrelling. I heard the two shots myself, around five o'clock, and then I heard it when the ambulance came. You know, Labaye junior loves fighting. A neighbour fought with him too, and Labaye can't wait to get back at him. He hasn't finished.

(10) Bedside Stories
So, it seems that (*"il paraît que"*) Bernard has a "dove." Seems they were seen passing by the other night.

...

So, it seems she's pregnant! Yes, it seems the son said so in the schoolbus, that he was going to have a little brother.

...

It seems that she brings him breakfast in bed every morning.

(11) The Source
P: Have there ever been lawsuits between people of the hamlet?
E: Oh, yes. There was one everyone talks about, between Aufrère and old Brigand. They shared a spring, a source of water, eight days for one, eight for the other. And then I think one of them kept it longer and the other filed a complaint. The judge asked Brigand, "How long have you seen the water running?" Brigand answered, "It's been running there for over 160 years." "And how old are you?" asked the judge. "Sixty," he answered. "All right, you may sit down." Ha ha ha.

(12) The Inheritance
D: So apparently Duchêne has inherited, did you know? Yes, the only son of an old aunt of his had gone to America. He was killed, stabbed by a knife, and sent back home embalmed in a sealed coffin

with a glass lid. So now Duchêne and his sisters are the only heirs of their aunt. I just saw him at the grocer.
P: Did *he* tell you?
D: No, of course not! And I couldn't very well congratulate him, he'd just think I wanted a part in it.

(13) Fields
This is where the fire was. Thérèse set it on fire herself so no one could ask her for her hay. Gilles wouldn't cut it, it was full of brambles. But because of the drought there wasn't much hay, and everyone had their eye on hers. So this bothered her a lot, and she set it on fire. So as not to have to give it to the first person who asked.

...

Thérèse let Colin use another of her fields; Gilles wasn't taking care of it and she was ashamed of leaving it unused. The Colin's cultivated it and had a very good harvest. And Madame Colin said, "I'm so embarrassed, everyone is jealous."

(14) *The Buzzard Chick and Other Hen Stories*
P: Didn't she have hens?
D: No, not the last couple of years. Some time ago she had just one small chicken left; the others had been taken by foxes or dogs. So she kept it with her in the kitchen. But as it got older, it started growing long claws, "like a buzzard," she said. I told her it was probably because she was keeping it inside. But she was sure it had been hatched in a buzzard's nest and fed by a buzzard, and was now growing into a buzzard-like monster. So she killed it and left it for the dogs. That was her last chicken.

...

Did I ever tell you about Mère Rigole? She lived right next to Thérèse's father when he was a child. Her house is just a dim ruin now, down the little road there. Well, every evening some hens would be missing at Thérèse's grandfather's house, and he would send his son to get them at Mère Rigole's house. Because every day she lured them into her house with some grain to make them lay their eggs there. And every evening Thérèse's father would be sent to ask her if she had seen their hens and she would yell, "*Quoi?* Your dirty hens, always running into my house and making a mess. Get them out of here!" Every day, all year round, they would repeat the same story.

(15) A Sister's Virtue
P: It seems Forêt was once a big town. It had the biggest market in the area, and a courthouse.
E: Oh, yes. One of my ancestors was even judged and sentenced to death there. He had a sister who was working as a maid for the lords of Chateauvilain. Every evening the Seigneur accompanied her halfway home. One day she got pregnant. So her brother, my ancestor, hid under the little bridge that crosses the brook, and when his sister and the Seigneur arrived, he jumped up and pushed the Seigneur into the brook.
P: And they sentenced him to death for that?
E: Well, the man died from the fall. So my ancestor ran away, all the way to Paris. But three, maybe four years later, they found him and he was hanged.

2.2 What the Stories Tell

This is only a selection of the many stories I was told. In the following analysis I will refer mainly to these stories, but the analysis is unavoidably based on the totality of stories I encountered. The aim is to become familiar with the types of topics and evaluations presented in the stories, but not to enter into an exhaustive literary analysis of them.

Apart from their potential to arouse the attention and curiosity of most human beings – myself included – with their dramatic and intriguing content, the stories that circulate about persons in and around the village are quite instructive on a number of different levels. Not only do they say something on an immediate level about relations between people in the village, but they also say something on another level and from a broader perspective about the mechanisms of "moral" evaluation and identification in general.

Furthermore, the specific stories being told, the way they are told and the variations they assume, all say something about the narrators and their relationships to the protagonists of those stories and to their audience. It is obvious that telling a story is not just mechanical recitation, but like all cultural performances, involves personal choices and contextual considerations, not to mention inventiveness, narrative skill and pleasure.

Characters

In general, the stories deal with what *others* do or have done. The narrator is thus never the main character, and the stories never bear reference to an experiencing subject. People only talk about themselves when it comes to illness and medical treatment, and I have never considered such accounts in my category of stories because they do not imply interpretation and evaluation of action, and because they, unlike the stories I did select, belong to the small domain of uninhibited talk (see Chapter 3).

Narrators always mask their sources. They even leave unsaid whether their information is first-, second- or "infinity-" hand. A formulation like "Pierre told me..." or "I noticed that..." is very rare. In fact, the overall rule is that the narrator is not a witness, be it direct or indirect: the story comes from someone else, who heard it from yet another person. The narrator him/herself may appear in a story to confirm the accuracy of an incident by having witnessed something in relation to it. But narrators have always witnessed only side-effects or small parts of an event – e.g., having seen it was a good cow (9), hearing gunshots and sirens (10B) – if anything at all. They never witness the event itself, occurring as it often does in the private sphere. Furthermore, personal observations do not always *in themselves* confirm the specific story from the point of view of logic – the girl always went to church (1A), she passed in front every morning (6) – although they are probably meant to, according to simple causality. Such observations are just as much narrative effects, adding to the suspense.

My remarks are not intended to discredit the stories, only to determine their nature. In many cases, the narrator has actually witnessed more than he or she admits, but chooses to remain vague about his/her own participation. Either underplaying or enhancing the accuracy of a narrative is always done in light of discretion, as if to leave room for doubt, in a skilful balance between assurance and uncertainty. This balance could be characterized as one of the paradoxes of stories.

Doubt and secrecy of sources is typically preserved by introductions like: "So, it seems that…" (*Alors, il paraît que…*), and, "They say…" (*On dit que…, ils disent que…*).[2] On the few occasions when I asked where or whom certain information or a particular story came from, my question was ignored. Again, valid though it may be, information is infused with a tinge of uncertainty that takes on the qualities of reversibility. Uncertainty far exceeds the domain of True versus False ("Did he really do that?"), opening onto a moral system of personal interpretation and non-definitive evaluation and identification that is very far from the stereotype image of harsh judgment and stubbornly fixed values attributed to rural societies. The paradoxical nature of the stories mentioned above has to do with the paradox of the moral system in

---

2 "*Alors?*" (So…?) even implies that the listener is obviously already informed, diminishing the image of the narrator as a "*pipelette*," a newsmonger, and heightening the feeling of conspiracy.

general: that people are constantly evaluated but never judged in the irreversible and stigmatizing sense of the word. This will be further illustrated.

We have said the stories deal with what others go about doing, but not just *any* others. A story about an unknown person is not liable to rouse more than vague interest. If there is no relationship, good or bad, there is no story. This can be pictured as a kind of fluctuating auto-centric social "sphere" around every individual, composed of good, bad and other relations that are more (though never entirely) neutral. This sphere could also be called the individual's "field of tension." Outside this field, relations are without meaning or even non-existent. Two persons will exchange stories only where their fields overlap, not beyond. Inversely, if there is no knowledge about a person, there is probably no relation, and this of course goes both ways. This could in fact provide a definition of rumours as stories dealing with events and people outside both the narrator's and the audience's fields of tension, and thus outside their field of influence. As such, the definition is not, as usual, based on the content of the stories nor on their truthfulness, but on *relational distances* contextual to their telling.

Relational distance or proximity determines the stories' existence and relevance. In terms of subject, just as there is "too far," there is also "too close." The avoidance of talking about oneself extends to the near family, that is, to the family unit living and working together. Close kin such as siblings, parents' siblings and first cousins,[3] and very close friends and allies are also avoided, but less stringently, and depending on the quality of the relation, so to speak. Story-topics thus seem to form a continual line stretching from oneself into the unknown, "too hot" at one end and "too cold" at the other. As we shall see, no one but the individual him/herself ever has a fixed place on this line: most social relations are quite fluctuating and malleable, meaning that a person suddenly can become "tepid" or distant enough to be a topic or, inversely, can heat up and get too close to be talked about.

---

3   This term will be used to distinguish children of siblings from relatives in general, also called *"cousins,"* despite the fact that the explicit terms for first cousins (*cousins germains* or *cousins issus de germains*) are rarely employed in La Brumaire.

Once the character in a story has been identified, directly or indirectly, his or her name is not generally mentioned again. This is probably partly to show discretion (one never knows who might be listening), but it can also be interpreted as a kind of "supernatural" protection of the people discussed, as though mentioning a name too often might make that person vulnerable to external powers. In the beginning of my stay, I did not always understand who the subject of conversation was. But when asked to repeat the name, most people ignored the question or, if they could not, whispered it quickly, obviously ill at ease.

In sum, stories are never about the narrator him/herself but about *known* people that are *not too close*. The sources are hidden and the information conveyed is invested with discretion and non-stigmatizing doubt.

Themes
As a general principle, the stories deal with what others do or have done: theft, incest, death, murder, suicide, pyromania, spellcasting, adultery, fighting, (the abuse of) inheritance, etc. – deliberate actions in most cases.[4] The characterization of a person is rarely presented directly, but preferably expressed through an account of something he or she has done, letting deeds speak for themselves.

Apart from the obvious, the stories contain a variety of different themes that can only be established by examining them more closely and comparing them. These themes offer preliminary insight into some of the conditions of coexistence, an insight that will be further developed in the coming chapters.

(1) The Child in the Dunghill:
This story is presented in four more-or-less different versions, with a number of recurring elements. Repetition is of course the basic condition

---

4 Even accidents are not always considered completely innocent. They are often coupled with a certain idea of fault and moral causality, as in the story of a man, who caused his mother's and niece's death because he wouldn't share some mushrooms with his road companions, and later went back to get them in the dark, overlooking that some of them were *amanitae*. The family stew did not kill *him*.

for considering the accounts to be one and the same story, and discussing them thereafter as variations. This is obviously an analytical choice, although I think if asked, the different contributors would agree they were talking about "the same thing." The fact that versions do not always concur is important for understanding the mechanisms of personal interpretation and silence. Furthermore, elements that recur and impose themselves indicate their own importance as key elements, especially when they are interpreted in different and even opposite ways. The following points were noted:

– An infant has presumably been killed. In two versions this is not commented upon, but taken for granted, which seems to imply that infanticide is or has been so commonplace that it does not even warrant discussion. The killing itself is not the crime; it is a private matter and does not directly concern the neighbours.

– Odour is vested with great significance: in one version the smell is prevented from spreading (with ashes), in the other its dissemination is central to the crime, if not the crime itself: the smell of evil imposes itself on bypassers and also leads to the discovery. Odour figures as something that must be controlled, precisely because it is elusive and uncontrollable. It escapes from one person's private domain and enters another's, betraying the emitter and intimidating the receiver. It also enters the public domain through dispersal: entering several "privates" and being subject to talk. Odour thus says something important about trespassing the private zone and violating distances that should be respected. And it highlights the tension of private and public existing between houses, families, persons. As we shall see later, sounds and noises have some of the same characteristics, emanating from households when not well controlled, and publicly bestowing others with knowledge. As regards knowledge and knowing, the intricate borderline between private and public could be articulated as follows: that information about someone's private matters is known by someone else does not make such knowledge public. Only when it is *known* that someone knows does the knowledge become public (within the village, that is). Following the same logic, the private could be defined as everything one doesn't wish to know about others *publicly*. Everyone had seen that the girl was pregnant, and then that she was not, but odour alone afforded them public, unequivocal certainty of the situation. This transition of private matters into public knowledge is obviously accentuated when the knowledge in question concerns matters that are violations of official law. I will develop this issue later.

– In two versions, the law and the church – two external and powerful institutions – forgive and condone something they consider a crime, and the village, polluted by smell and by "knowing," is left the task of judging.

– In Version A, the condemnation/acceptance paradox is very clear. As we have seen, the issue of the baby's demise is deemed irrelevant. So on one hand, we have the spread of evil through odour, and on the other, the fact that the girl is hard-working. Somehow these two aspects counterbalance each other evenly in this particular version. That does not leave us with a neutral story devoid of evaluation, however. Without overtly condemning or accepting the action, everyone listening and telling (or not telling) nevertheless takes a stance, literally positioning themselves in a certain place in the social landscape vis-à-vis the family in question.

– The fourth version is told by someone who clearly wishes to protect the family: the narrator dismisses any derogatory utterances or stories about them, although he is obviously well aware of what others say. By the same token, he expresses his gratitude to the family, who helped him start up a business after the war by using his services. Clearly, he does not judge or condemn them in his account, nor does he refrain from telling similar stories about other neighbours. It follows that his motivations are not of a moral, but of a relational, order.

– The question of names is worth mentioning. In Version A, the girl is identified by her mother's maiden name, Dubois, not her own surname. This is obviously an allusion to a number of other stories that call the reputation of the mother's family into question. Using this name thus draws a parallel between the stories, reinforcing the credibility of one story (and thus its teller) with the others, and vice versa. The father is often described as coming from a respectable family, polluted by his regrettable marriage. In Version B, the storytellers choose to identify the girl as a Pelletier, probably to locate the place (the father's shop), and because they thought the specification "Dubois" would not mean anything to me anyway. They are quite surprised (and worried) that I am aware of the reputation of a family which they know I have not had the opportunity to relate to. They are mainly interested in relation to the priest, discussing the local case in terms of a story in the newspapers about a Catholic priest who stabbed a woman carrying his child – another story involving a priest and the death of a baby.

The sum of all these stories creates a new, all-encompassing, virtual story that constitutes a kind of "total public knowledge" of the affair. Each interpreter picks out elements for his or her private version, omitting some, adding others, and these different versions colour each other. In my interpretation, I have mixed the elements of all versions, concluding that the infant was actually killed (i.e., that for one thing there *was* a dead infant, and for another it did not die naturally), even though three versions do not overtly state this. A fourth version, coupled with background knowledge of the local incidence of infant-killings, leads me to come to this conclusion.

I draw two types of conclusions: like anyone hearing stories, I draw conclusions about the persons involved, and what actually happened, mixing what I hear together with what I have heard elsewhere. I also compare versions to deduce something about what one omits and another includes, and thus about silences. This procedure is debatable, but probably the only one possible when dealing with silence, and when resorting to lie detectors or other more verifiable methods is inappropriate. It is certain, though, that the people talking were just as aware of other versions as I was; they made implicit allusion to them, thus giving meaning to their own silences.

(2) The Thieving Family
– The father/husband is from an "honest family." He has married into a family of thieves, and their bad character somehow reflects on him, although he is to a certain extent considered separately by the locals. The others, on the other hand, are considered together with bad characteristics that are hereditary. This is confirmed in other stories about the family. (As a general principle, character traits, usually bad ones, can be attributed to whole families.) Another family is considered "bad" (*mauvais*) because one of the uncles has a grandchild who is in prison for murder: an "assassin," a stain on the family honour (*Ça tâche, ça, pour la famille*). This phenomenon obviously contradicts the principle of not attributing definite properties to anyone.

– About the grammar of stealing and thieves: degrees of malevolence can be conveyed here depending on the choice of terminology, some more serious and threatening than others. The verbal form *ils volaient* (they stole) and the adjectival form *ils étaient voleurs* (they were thievish, or thieving) are employed in these variations, not the substantive form, *ç'étaient des voleurs* (they were thieves). The latter, being a thief, would sound more definitive and irreversible than simply being thieving. Stealing, *voler*, is an activity that is delimited in time (doing: syntagmatic). The substantive forms, *voleur* and *voleuse* (thief) indicate an inherent trait or condition, something irreversible (being: paradigmatic). The adjectival form, *être voleur* (to be thievish), indicates a manner, a reversible quality, a way of being. The narrators' use of softened language reinforces the earlier idea of flexibility and non-stigmatization in their evaluation and identification of others, and heightens their paradoxical relation to the indelible "family stain."

"We were more ashamed than they." As in the case of odour bestowing knowledge and complicity upon the neighbours, the witnesses of the thievish family were embarrassed mainly by knowing. If the family wanted to steal, they should have done it more discreetly, keeping it their own (and their victims') business. The stealing itself does not make the story worthwhile, the discovery of it and the woman's shameless response does.

(3) The Young Girl in the Storm at *le Gâtinet*
This story is amusing mainly for the way it is told. The first part is presented with no notion of time, as though the event just took place. Recounted to an old woman as a recent event, it appears to have taken place about seventy-five years ago, before the first narrator was even born. But it has become part of the timeless *corpus* of local stories and of the place it happened, forever written in the soil of *le Gâtinet*.

(4) The Bastard Goes to his Father's Wedding
– The two versions do not contradict each other, but the person telling Version B does not go into detail, although she is obviously aware of the incident in the church. Instead, she immediately identifies the characters in relation to herself, advising me this way not to pursue the matter and say something I could regret.

– In Version A, the main event of the story is not that Chavenaud has made two girls pregnant at the same time, nor that the son of the Dumas girl is illegitimate (an *enfant naturel*) – such things happen all the time. The main event, and what makes the story, is that the Dumas girl shows up in church with the baby, accompanied by her father. Such indiscretion, so direct a "discourse," is rare.

(5) The Window
This story somehow speaks for itself. If we take it matter-of-factly, someone killed a teenager, presumably because she had a physical handicap. But it took place within the private sphere and was nobody else's business. The story refrains from making any direct moral evaluation of the action, although obviously it plays on, and somehow defies, the general edict, "Thou shall not kill." Nevertheless, it seems that because the child was handicapped, it will always be possible to throw suspicion on the parents. Just a few words are sufficient to do this.

(6) The Brigand Sisters
– This is a lovely story about events that took place back in the twenties but still impinge on relations today. The conflicts of the two families, today presided over by the grandchildren of the Brigand sisters, dominate the atmosphere of the hamlet, rendering the ambiance quite tense. Their lands were once unified by their common great-grandfather Brigand, who must have been an important man locally. But each party seems to suspect the other of wanting to restore and occupy the position of their forefather as leader of the hamlet and its lands. Today, the two parties share rather ambivalent relations, reflecting both positive and negative sides of their common origin. Furthermore, the complicated brother/half-brother/cousin paradox tops things off: despite the obvious tension and suspicion, they have bought land and farming equipment together, and they help each other in all major agricultural tasks, incorporating a third partner who is neutral in family matters. Until the land reallotment interfered, their joint venture apparently sustained a balanced situation of mutual and controlled interdependence. But with the new conflict, the negative sides of their relations have been reactivated with an intensity that gives the impression they were just waiting for a chance to resurface. In any case, the

delicate balance has been disturbed by the land reallotment, which is of unknown amplitude and directness and which belongs to an external form of discourse.

– In both versions, several allusions are made to the causes of the events. In Version A, the narrator almost suggests that sorcery was involved, or at least that the accidents were not natural. What strikes him is the fact that the two died exactly one year apart; the horse accident can be explained as an isolated incident, but the fact that the girl drops dead for no apparent reason on exactly the same day a year later immediately affects the first accident, changing its character from natural to unnatural. In Version B, the deaths are not associated with each other, and conflict is not evoked (it is "too close"), but the reason given for the girl's death is very particular and bears resemblance to certain religious taboos: she mixed milk and blood. The narrator does not actually know and cannot explain why mixing milk and blood is dangerous, but has probably heard the explanation often, and accepted it as valid.

I do not have a clear idea of what this mixing taboo is about either (although I do presume that it is "about something else"). But it is possible that where blood has to do with filiation defined through men, milk has to do with filiation through women. And where blood points to family or lineage, as a more abstract and timeless way of defining oneself, milk points to one's actual emergence in the world, inscribed in time. Blood is passed on and nourishes the family through time, whereas milk nourishes the individual in the immediate present. While it is clear that a person needs both to exist physically and socially, one is more physical, making the body grow and wet its diapers, and the other is more social, defining who one is. The woman who mixed the two not only mixed up abstract categories, but also actually fed her child her own blood, thus tampering with the paternal filiation of the child. This is only one hypothesis, however.

(7) The Jacket
This is a rather recent event, but, as the narrator says, it is already widely known. It is the kind of story that spreads like wildfire.

It can be noted that Fougère did not react when he saw his jacket, but discreetly left without claiming it. He would not have gone to ask for the jacket if he thought it had been stolen deliberately, and was surely ashamed of catching the other man red-handed like that. But the fact that the other denies everything although he has the jacket in his possession makes things clear. Claiming the jacket despite this denial would be like openly accusing the other of being a thief. Fougère prefers to buy another jacket – and tell the story, of course, illustrating the other's bad manners, as well as his own perfect management of a delicate situation.

(8) Riolet and the Cows
– A good example of a two-sided discourse. "No, people aren't superstitious here, they don't believe in spells, events aren't explained by sorcery" – whereupon the narrator engages in an unequivocal account of how Riolet threw one spell after another, and concludes with a return to "normality," to normal explanations. Despite the story's aspiration to rationality, the discourse of sorcery is present therein, and is apparently the preferred explanation. Rationality and sorcery do not contradict each other though. Rather, they complement each other in this case, the distinction between natural and unnatural faculties (*dons*) being vague and open to interpretation. The choice is left open to the audience – to me, in this case – and doubt is preserved.

– Somehow this framing or parenthesizing of sorcery in rational discourse consciously marks it as "other," warning me that we have entered another domain of discourse, perhaps that of the private, normally unsaid (*non-dit*) – in any case, the domain of the unofficial. Such framing is similar to the procedure undertaken in the very first story, where the account opens and ends with "Don't say anything (but)..." (*faut pas l'dire*), marking both the story, the narrator and the situation as exceptional. In any case, it is certain that sorcery is very rarely evoked, and most often in negating terms. If evoked, it is confirmed only in very special circumstances. But the discourse is undoubtedly there. The scenario here is very similar to that of the Norman Bocage described by Jeanne Favret-Saada (see Chapter 3.2).

– The narrator affirms that a car accident or the death of a calf does not necessarily imply that spells are involved. This confirms what Favret-Saada says: single events are not explained by sorcery. Only when they occur with unnatural frequency do people start suspecting the intervention of supernatural powers (1977: 233-36, 334). In La Brumaire, this is illustrated in the story of the Brigand sisters above, and reintroduced here. The first cow's sudden tractability in Riolet's hands is not itself attributed to sorcery, neither in the narrative nor probably in the original reasoning of the events when they happened. But when a second cow changes character after passing through Riolet's hands, the first event goes up for review. The consecutive occurrence of similar events cinches the affair: Riolet has unnatural powers, and he exploits them for his own purposes and against his neighbours.

(9) Labaye's Eye
– In the process of establishing an inventory of landowners whose property lay within the perimeter of the land reallotment, I was told stories like this one: "Labaye and his father are no longer on speaking terms for this and that reason, but his father can still be counted as being against." It would not surprise anyone if Labaye senior was for the reallotment considering his pre-existing conflict with his son, who is overtly against. Being "for" would be an opportune occasion for him to publicly express and even emphasize his opposition towards his son.
   – Labaye did not lodge a complaint against his father, and the judicial event withered away. This is the general picture as far as I can discover: only very few complaints about violation of the law are lodged, and always by public servants or the police. This is what happened in the story of the child in the dunghill, but the investigations had no further consequences for the implicated persons. In another instance, a house burned for the fourth time in about ten years, and this time the insurance company asked the police to investigate the matter. It was determined that the fire was criminal: newspapers and an empty petrol tank had been found inside the locked house. Everyone had their own theory, but no one was ever officially charged. In another case, a person lodged charges after a fight against someone carrying weapons (*contre X pour porte d'arme*), not specifying whom he was accusing. "I didn't give him away, eh. I didn't want to. Even if they're right-wing, those guys are from around here, eh. We get along fine now." (*Je l'ai pas vendu, hein. Je voulait pas le vendre, même s'ils sont de droite, ce sont des gars du pays, hein. – On est bien ensemble maintenant*). Finally, the surveyor in charge of the land reallotment filed charges against "X" for removing his expensive orange landmarks, and the members of the Association against the reallotment were all summoned by the police. But no one

was accused since there was no evidence, only "hearsay" (and the police, unlike other investigators, need proof).

– The two versions do not contradict one another, but B refines A a bit, dividing the responsibility between father and son. Still, Labaye junior with his love for fighting is treated with great respect and humour. In general, expressing yourself with your fists is preferable to speaking, is considered more noble and, strangely enough, less direct, less unmasking than using words. It is another kind of discourse – it is "doing."

(10) Bedside Stories
– Everyone has seen Bernard drive past with the girl late at night, everyone talks about it. But everyone also closes windows and shutters at sundown, not letting the slightest glimpse of light escape and betray their privacy. In the village and hamlets in the evening, an almost frightening lifelessness reigns. But apparently there is more to it than meets the eye. Everyone sees everything, everyone has seen Bernard and the girl...

– Children are a useful source of knowledge about others because people might be less careful about what they say in their presence. At the same time, until children learn to mind their tongue, they are a dangerous source of knowledge about their *own* home and family, and must be well trained not to violate familial privacy. In this story, not only does the boy talk too much, but the other children nicely retain the information and repeat it to their parents. That is how I heard it: through a child who told it to her parents who told it to a grandmother who told it to a neighbour who told me. *Et voilà, tout le monde sait.*

– She brings him breakfast in bed... How on earth did that information get out? Maybe through the same channels, maybe through the baker, in whose shop she accidentally let it slip, or maybe it was invented elsewhere. In any case, it is the kind of intimate knowledge that everyone would want to keep private if it were about themselves, but enjoy knowing when it's about others. It is in no way intimidating knowledge, it is not particularly mean, it says nothing about their characters, good or bad, except that he is well treated, maybe even a bit spoiled. The whole point of knowing is...knowing.

The standard formula, "It seems..." (*il paraît que...*), is consistently employed to leave the field open for interpretation and to mask sources.

The neutral or passive form, "They saw him go by," or "He was seen..." (*on l'a vu passer*) is used rather than "I saw him," or "Claude saw him" (*je l'ai vu*, or *Claude l'a vu*).

(11) The Spring
– While it is true that people rarely engage in judicial proceedings, there is one exceptional kind of offence that immediately leads to lawsuits: when private property, rights to water and right of passage are violated. According to the story, Brigand reacted very quickly after the violation of his rights. During my stay, several cases went to court: a nephew had been suing his uncle for years for a strip of about two square metres of land running alongside the nephew's house and giving the uncle access to his own back yard. According to the land register and two preceding trials, the land actually belonged to the uncle, and it was obviously a symbolic case more than anything else, since the land was of absolutely no use to the nephew. This was probably the revival of an old conflict, the nephew symbolically claiming his right to the whole property.

In another case, the problem of tenancy was brought to court when a tenant, who had freely given up his lease so the owner could exploit the land himself, finally would not leave, and demanded that the lease be re-established. In another, a farmer had deviated the course of a stream, cutting it off and leaving the farm downstream, which was owned by an old woman, without its free, natural water supply. Many people were hoping for a lawsuit, both because they were indignant on behalf of the defenceless woman, and because the farmer in question was the Mayor, and the instigator of the land reallotment. This was an occasion to tell him he could not get away with everything.

Finally, someone let the water out of my mother-in-law's millpond, washing away the fish, and she was encouraged to raise charges *contre X*. Disappointed when she refused, people were then somewhat reassured by the fact that one uninhibited village personality, Gaby, would surely spread the news around: *"Gaby le dira bien un peu partout..."* All these examples give the impression that lawsuits serve first and foremost as public expressions of people's positions and opportunities to publicize their opponents' outrageous conduct, and that being the object of such attention is a stronger penalty than any judge could inflict.

– The event described took place before the narrator was born, i.e., around the turn of the century. (He remembers that when he was five years old, he visited Brigand, who was old and confined to his bed.) Brigand was thus born around 1840. The story has taken the form of a tale of the old days, and has probably lost its immediate social context. Brigand's name has withered away, the only two Brigand's living there in 1954 were old and unmarried, and the Tisseront's are gone too. Therefore, the story does not say anything important about any living person, it is a reminiscence about a former social landscape. Its relevance today seems to be that one should mind one's words: Brigand talked too much, exaggerated in court and was publicly ridiculed. Furthermore, telling the story establishes the narrator as someone with roots in the hamlet. And finally, it is a good story that makes people laugh.

(12) The Inheritance
It is of course interesting to know that Duchêne has inherited something, but we don't know what or how much. In fact, the real, rich part of the inheritance is this spectacular and exotic story about the aunt's son... Killed (like a gangster)! Embalmed (like an Egyptian pharaoh)! And put into the most extraordinary American coffin! These details will be remembered and cherished for a *long* time.

(13) Fields
Two stories about neighbourly jealousy, about having "too much."
– Thérèse set fire to her field so as not to have to give the hay to someone with whom she did not want to be in an exchange relation. Since she herself was not harvesting it, she had "too much," and had someone asked for it directly, she could not have said no. But if she gave it to one person, all the other neighbours and allies would be terribly offended. The easiest way out of her predicament was to get rid of the hay in a neutral way. Nobody could reproach her for that. As it was, the fire burned quite uncontrollably and could easily have spread to other fields, but that was a minor risk compared to the former one, offending neighbours. In any case, after the fire she was safe: she again had "just enough" (*tout juste assez*).
– Negligence is generally resented and avoided, and Thérèse preferred to let the Colin's use her field rather than leave it unexploited for one year, open for all to see. But the Colin's had a very good harvest on

that specific field, which was also open for all to see, and they felt ashamed. They were not paying for the land, any other neighbour might have disposed of the field just as well, and they were taking advantage of the fact that old Thérèse could not manage anymore. If they had had a good harvest on their own land or a moderate harvest on Thérèse's land, nobody would have cared. But in this specific constellation they had "too much."

"Taking advantage," *profiter*, is a recurring theme reflecting the idea of an unequal balance of exchange. "So, they're taking advantage, eh!" (*Ah! Ils en profitent, hein!*) People will do anything not to look as if they're taking advantage of someone else, of someone's weakness or misery. Recently a man was buried in the village cemetery, and after the funeral everyone would have gone to the bistro as they always do on such occasions, but the bistro was closed. The buried man had worked for the bistro owner's family and it would have been very indecent to "profit" from his funeral, as they said. "*Ça s' fait pas!*" – It's just not done. I was the only one who was surprised that it was closed, everyone else took it for granted.

It is said of a certain man that his happiness is built on the misfortune of others ("*Il a fait son bonheur sur le malheur des autres*"). The explanation is that he was an orphan from child welfare, and was taken in and eventually adopted by a couple who had another son of their own. This son was getting married and his fiancée was pregnant, but he was killed in a car accident and the adopted boy thus became the sole heir. Today, he is often called by his orphan name as a reminder of his origins and his unmerited luck. But it is not because he came from child welfare that people resent him. Other villagers have similar origins without having to hear about it. Rather, the person in question is considered arrogant, ill-tempered (*mauvais*) and mean to children. Again, there is a difference between stigmatizing someone and judging their actual behaviour. In this specific case there seems to be a bit of both: the man's orphan origins come in handy in emphasizing the judgment of his behaviour and determining that he has *profité* and now has "too much." But were he not orphan, another pretext would surely be found for accounting for his behaviour.

(14) The Buzzard Chick and Other Hen Stories
These two stories – one about a domesticated animal turning wild and one about an egg-snatching neighbour – are more than simple reflections on current affairs. They, like some of the other stories, deal with fundamental issues, and have more in common with fairytales or myths than with daily chit-chat. Or rather, they show how archetypal tales and myths are often an integral part of everyday communication.

Without having a real moral, the first of these stories contains the idea that if one is not careful and vigilant, then nature and wildness – in the form of a peaceable chicken transforming into a taloned, carnivorous buzzard – may sneak into hearth and home and threaten it from within. The chicken was killed and left to the dogs, not even considered edible. An analogy can be found in a current French rumour analyzed by J.-N. Kapferer, one I also heard, describing how ecologists have been throwing boxes of vipers into the fields from helicopters at night as a part of their fight against peasant farmers (*cultivateurs*), in order to bring the countryside back to its wild, natural state. The rumour coincides with European laws forcing farmers to lay land fallow in order to reduce their production. In the first, the story of the buzzard chick, nature intercalates itself; in the second, it is introduced by humans. But in both, the foundations of peasant life, domestication and cultivation, are threatened by what seem to be the eternal forces of nature – or its ambassadors – against agriculture and society. The same idea recurs in the valuation of work and the resentment of negligence, since negligence often results in vegetation growing wild and "nature taking over." Hence, an enormous amount of time and work is dedicated to maintaining fences and brooks and trimming hedges, trees and underbrush. And the mere idea of laying land fallow and unattended to, as recommended by EEC guidelines, is revolting to Brumairians. Nature is a force that must be fought constantly and peasant farmers are our main defenders.

The second story relates how a set of neighbours established a system of unofficial exchange: a woman who apparently had no chicken of her own, received a couple of eggs every day from her neighbours without getting them openly as a gift, an arrangement that would call for compensation. The story thus shows how, without engaging in the commitment of open exchange, one can nevertheless express neighbourly tolerance, even if the neighbour is not an ally. The appropriation of the eggs could have been considered theft, just as the theft of milk in Story 2 was. But instead of creating or reinforcing conflict, the chicken-owners chose to remain indulgent, obliged to do so by proximity. And their descendants chose to tell the story, showing how their forefathers upheld a state of ceasefire with this close neighbour, a relationship that was neither allied nor conflictual, but not neutral either. The story again articulates the tense and ambiguous relations of neighbourhood, of intermingling private spheres, and its contrast with the milk-thief story shows how these relations often hang by a slender thread.

(15) A Sister's Virtue
Intrigued to discover what is known of an old town that was once quite important and now almost completely vanished, with only a few ruins and the remains of a cobblestone street to reveal its location to those who already know it, I talked to an old friend, wishing to hear what he could say about the last inhabitants. But mentioning the name clearly brings up memories far more important than those of a distant village with which he had no contact: it conjures memories of a heroic forefather. For my friend, the town is significant mainly as a place where an unjust and external law was enforced. This story, like the earlier ones, is mainly interesting for its fairytale and almost myth-like features which will be analyzed in Chapter 2.4.

2.3 Telling Stories: Conditions and Situations

As has already been mentioned, talking in La Brumaire is generally extremely restricted, and the virtues of silence and discretion are often emphasized. But stories nevertheless circulate. The question is, what are the conditions of their circulation, and in what situations, under which circumstances, by whom and to whom, are they told? This is the general subject of Chapter 3; here I will just mention some more "behaviouristic" aspects of the actual telling of stories.

All the stories cited were told to me directly or, in some cases, to a larger public in my presence. If stories are written down here, it is because I heard them. This might seem banal, but it is important in many ways. My sources are stories repeated to me by someone – a neighbour, friend, the postman, my mother-in-law – at an often unknown (social) distance from the events recalled (n^{th} hand). The stories are not just pulled out of a pool of common village knowledge. They emerge in a specific form on a specific occasion, involving specific persons.

As I have already said, I was often told a story so that I could understand relational matters in the village, like family connections, conflicts or alliances. But I was armed with such knowledge only because I already had a specific and well-defined position in current village matters. I was not neutral, I was not an "outsider" (nor an "insider"), I was someone who had a reason for being there and for knowing. I had a clearly established, and hence negotiable, position. For a story is only told once the interlocutor has been identified, that is, when people think they know to whom they are talking. Furthermore, the general situation must be surveyed: who else is around, who might be listening or, if too far away to hear, watching the exchange?

The specific social position of every interlocutor in current village affairs must also be taken into consideration, and the story adjusted accordingly. Telling a story to someone thus requires being up-to-date. And according to the social identity of the receiver, some story elements may be left out, others explained in detail, and yet others exaggerated.

A story is never told arbitrarily or just for fun, there is always a reason for it. Reasons can be quite varied: to get something in exchange, to include someone in a circle, to warn someone, to make someone laugh, to discredit someone, to explain something such as another incident, to expose or clarify one's relationship to those talked about, those listening, etc. And such reasons are always manifold, and never determinable with certainty.

An atmosphere of intimacy always prevails when stories are told. This is a pre-requisite for, but also a result of, telling stories. People will take a rapid glance around them, lower their voices, move subtly towards each other so as to close the circle, still glancing around, and then commence storytelling. Any external sound, like a car, a tractor or a pedestrian passing by outside, will provoke some uneasiness and a short break in the account, which is taken up again when the source of interruption, whose every movement has been followed closely by everyone present, is out of range again.

However familiar I was with the signs announcing the imminent exposure of important information, I was sometimes surprised by the casualness with which quite disturbing knowledge was unveiled. Obviously, what might have seemed casual to me was, of course, just as controlled as the more intimately framed revelations were, I just wasn't prepared for it. I mention it here to stress that storytelling was a part of daily conversation and could not always be assimilated into the almost ritual exchanges described above, although even in the most casual settings, relations between those present were necessarily already inscribed in a system of exchange. I will return with more detail to the circumstances of exchange shortly.

2.4 Stories and Myths

Some of the stories above have an almost myth-like character. They seem to carry significance and perpetuate themselves the same way myths do, and they not only describe actual events, they also say something more generally about communal life.

Chapter 2.2 deals with "what the stories tell" on different analytical and semiotic levels, looking equally at their actual content (e.g., Labaye and his father no longer speaking to one another), at more general elements of coexistence (e.g., scent betrays things, and judgment is not irreversible), and at what telling a story a certain way indicates about relations between its protagonists and those telling and listening (e.g., A shows B he has esteem for C by *not* telling a certain story about C).

Some of the classical definitions of myths in the literature are based on content only. Eliade defines myths as accounts of supernatural cosmological creation (Eliade 1963: 16-17), and Lévi-Strauss as stories from the time when humans and animals were not yet distinct (Lévi-Strauss and Eribon 1988: 193-95). These contributors are obviously inspired, and in some cases limited, in their definitions by the objects of their own analysis. Barthes' approach is more liberal, and furthermore requires that form be added to content. Everything can be a myth according to him, as long as "a type of social usage...is added to pure matter" (Barthes 1973: 109). His interest in form emerges mainly in his definition of myth as "a type of speech, a form" (ibid.), and his statement that the repetition of things makes him think they are significant (ibid.: 12).

I also identify odour as a key element because its mention recurs – attracting attention even though, or rather because, its representation is reversed in different versions (escaping versus being contained). But from noting this recurrence, the analysis necessarily moves on to its *raison d'être*, the content, to the meaning of "odour." One can be guided by form, but only as a preliminary to signification. Treating repetition this way was inspired by my material itself, and not by a method consciously borrowed somewhere else and applied to it. This treatment nevertheless coincides with Barthes' approach, and is also similar to the way Lévi-Strauss treats differences between mythical versions, or inversions. As he says, a myth is constituted of all its variations, and sees the eventual analysis of a myth as yet another version of it

(Lévi-Strauss and Eribon 1988: 196). The more variations, the greater the chance of finding its structuring laws (Lévi-Strauss 1955: 92-94).

In *La voie des masques* (1979), Lévi-Strauss tries to follow the historical diffusion of different mythical characters and traits, both in myths and masks, among different Indian groups on the northwest coast of North America. He constantly encounters the same elements, often turned upside down, which makes them all the more interesting for his analysis. I acknowledge that in my interpretation, the dissemination or containment of odour, respectively signifying the leakage or control of information, resembles a Lévi-Straussian *"mythème"* (Lévi-Strauss 1955). But the difference between his approach and mine is that where he seeks structuring laws, a grammar that generates different versions, I go the opposite direction, gathering what I find in the stories into an overall, statistical model that does not exist in that form in daily life. The difference between these two approaches also reflects the main differences between Lévi-Strauss's and Ardener's perceptions of structure, as far as I can see (cf. Ardener 1978: 90-91).

I am not claiming that when people in La Brumaire talk about their neighbours, they are recounting myths. But I see some parallels between myths and stories, both in the way they can be analyzed and in the way they are perpetuated. Furthermore, as we have seen in some of the stories, mythical elements can be parts of daily talk, and the forms should not necessarily be dissociated.

To "de-mythstify" myths a little, I should say I think that, essentially, they are good stories. They convey important meaning, they are remembered, told and retold, and every time, they are interpreted and adapted to current situations. That is how they stay alive and why they vary. As Lévi-Strauss acknowledged recently, he has never actually been able to find either the common myth-generating structure or the grammatical rules of transformation that he was searching for (Lévi-Strauss & Eribon 1988: 197-98). What is left of Lévi-Strauss's theory of myth is, according to Sperber, cognitive interpretation and mnemonic selection, but that has nothing to do with "grammar," a device that engenders the totality of the formulations of a language (Sperber 1973: 115).

I think that what goes for myths, goes for the stories: they are remembered, told and retold because they carry information important to the people telling and listening to them. Some stories will be remembered for many years to come, others will eventually be forgotten and disappear because they have lost importance, like the story about the spring: Tisseront still remembers it, but I doubt if it will be told much longer (except by me, since the story carries another type of information – about itself – in my analysis).

In one story that I omitted, a person set fire to a neighbour's barn, making it look as though a tramp had been sleeping in the barn and had caused the fire. The person was caught though, and even went to jail for a while. The story goes that he wanted to buy the farm in question, but his neighbour would not sell it, so the man wanted revenge. The event took place at least a hundred years ago, and the farmowner in the story was a great-grandfather of a man who is seventy today. About thirty or forty years ago, some descendents of the "fire-setter" were teasing a neighbour, who addressed them with the nickname "the Firesetter's" (*famille de metteu' de feu*) which has been popular ever since. As people say today, "*Ah, ça résonne!*" – the name resonates, it will not be forgotten, like the story it refers to. Apparently it is still meaningful; it says something important about the family in question, and about the fact that they have never been able to shed the bad reputation of their forefather. As we have seen with so many other stories, the story carries information on several levels: specifically, that the members of that family are not totally trustworthy; and more generally, the message, "be careful what you do," a story will stick to you and your descendants for generations to come.

The story of revenging a sister's virtue (17) also has myth-like features; the narrator even refers to the main character as an ancestor. It is an important story about a time when lords had the supreme power and could do as they pleased, and about a hero who challenged this authority in the rightful name of family honour. It is thus about a time when local relations where still master/subject. Later the hierarchy was overthrown by the Revolution and in theory relations became horizontal. In this sense, the event took place in a mythical time different from today.[5] I doubt the narrator would be able to trace his relation to his

---

5 A mythical time "before men became equal" here substitutes for Lévi-Strauss's mythical time "when humans and animals were one" (*op.cit.*).

ancestor or even date the event approximately – it happened in some distant and unknown past to an unspecified ancestor. On the other hand, he can situate the scene of the action very precisely. The killing took place in what in those days was the uncharted "no-man's land" between the domains of two lords,⁶ and the ancestor was executed at Forêt, a town now withered away and covered with brush.

Coming back to the question of definitions, in light of these comments, an adequate definition of myth or mythical elements would certainly differ from the classical definitions above which seek to reduce the mythical field temporally to the time of creation or the time before human-animal separation. In my definition, mythicality would instead designate all (oral) manifestations expressing the fundamental principles of social existence, in this case, the relations between people and households, and the interplay between their inter-dependence and their autonomy.

---

6 Certain hamlets have names that associate the word "*brousse*," underbrush, with the name of a neighbouring village, (e.g., Brousse-Vernet), giving the impression that they lie in what was once a dark, dangerous zones of transition, controlled by neither of the two adjacent domains.

2.5 Conclusion

To sum up:

– Stories serve as social identifiers, positioning the implied persons – the characters, the narrators, the listeners – in relation to one another. They delineate and interpret the current social landscape.

– Stories always convey information on more than the immediate level of the people and events being accounted for.

– There are always reasons for telling a story, and they are never told to just anyone, anywhere. Often they are told as part of an exchange of knowledge, consolidating the relation between giver(s) and receiver(s).

– Stories never condemn characters irreversibly, and often contain contradictory information, so as to leave an opening for uncertainty and doubt, in a kind of balanced, non-definitive way.

– Some stories establish stains, *tâches*, that modify and diminish reversibility.

– Stories deal with the appropriate distances between people and families, marking out private and public spheres. They demonstrate how the terms "public" and "private" are constantly given new content, new scope, according to the issues at hand, and are thus relative terms, redefined for and by every new application.

– Stories reveal the extent of local knowledge about others. The fact that actions are never condemned even when they obviously violate official laws says something about distance from the official system, "here" being far away.

– Stories say something about the importance of others' actions and their influence on neighbours' lives. Stories deal with and evaluate people's conduct, and thus apparently deal with morality and rules. But rather than consolidating the limits of orderly conduct as might be expected (e.g., by declaring transgressions), stories eloquently demonstrate instead how such limits are constantly being shifted, replaced and restated in individual interpretations. The stories thus give clues to, and are themselves examples of, the ongoing evaluation and re-evaluation of other people based on their actions.

3

Exchanging Words

In La Brumaire, communication is subject to very strict rules, and the ongoing quest for silence and discretion is especially remarkable. These two communicational parameters are difficult to discern clearly because they are, obviously, not always expressed overtly. Nevertheless, it took me less than two weeks in the village to understand the importance of mastering them, one lying in the domain of talking, the other in the domain of action in general.

Initially, these parameters seem to contradict what we saw in the foregoing chapter: that a great deal of information circulates in the village about its inhabitants, and that everyone knows everything. This necessarily implies that people *do* talk, that they are not always silent. Thus, under certain circumstances, the norms of silence are breached. These "certain circumstances" will be analyzed here.

As I said before, exposing one's knowledge is a very cherished part of social life. Of course, this has nothing to do with the copious, almost excessive talking that goes on in the French capital of Paris, where silence is perceived as a lack of affirmation of one's identity. In La Brumaire, people *do* talk, and talking *is* a way of affirming one's identity, but so is silence. In the village, silence has a much broader range of expression and is much more developed and nuanced. It is almost a language in itself.

But the relationship between silence and speech is not one of norms versus praxis – i.e., people saying one thing and doing another. Rather, silence and speech have a paradoxical relationship, both being equally important, sometimes even simultaneous, complementary communicational parameters. To approach the paradox, let us assume that talking in La Brumaire is very meticulously measured and controlled. The aim will then be to describe this control, the ways of "not-talking," and to look closer at the circumstances under which the quest for silence is breached, considering that there is a kind of point of balance, where the alternation between silence and talk takes on the qualities of an exchange that in itself engenders meaning on a level other than the immediate one.

3.1 Silence and Discretion

Before developing a description, I would like to make some general and defining remarks about silence.

First of all, "silence" should be understood here in the communicational sense as representing the unsaid, *le non-dit*, not as the more abstract environmental-acoustic silence, "0 dB," that reigns over, for instance, a distant, deserted valley. For our purposes, only the silence conveyed by people is of relevance.

Secondly, silence may be devoid of sound, but it is not devoid of meaning: it is a form of communication, and can be considered the common signifier of everything unsaid. Thus, only in its acoustic properties is silence opposed to talking, in the same way that giving and not-giving (withholding) are both concrete elements of exchange. Silence and talking both indicate something about the relationship between subjects, tellers, audience, and more generally, about the principle of exchange. Silence is thus more than just the necessary intervals of non-meaning between words and syllables/phonemes making them discernible as such. Silence carries meaning just as much as words do. When Marc Augé talks about the power of words, he includes both those spoken and those implied, i.e., silent, *non-dits* (Lecture 25/6-91). He thus confirms the idea that silence is part of, not contrary to, speaking, and can be just as powerful.

Thirdly, the silence described here implies knowing, possessing something known. If a person does not "have" knowledge, his or her silence is insignificant;[1] there is nothing unsaid, no withholding going on. Silence, like exchange in general, requires having something, however basic – goods, daughters, knowledge. Within this frame of analysis, silence is having, but withholding. It is an essential part of the dynamic of word-exchange.

Finally, I do not find it useful to operate with the common and somehow artificial binary opposition with talking on one side, and silence and all other implicit forms of communication on the other (the

---

1 Or rather, as it could be phrased in a semiotic play on words, it is a sign (signifiant) of ignorance, of not-knowing.

"verbal versus non-verbal communication" dichotomy). Talking, silence, mimicry, gesticulation and action in general all constitute signs in a complicated system of interpersonal communication that functions, furthermore, on various (meta-)levels. Talking can, as we shall see, be just as "implicit" as in the case of mimicking, and so drawing a sharp distinction between verbal/explicit and non-verbal/implicit carries the current study no further, neither on a descriptive nor on an analytical level. If such a distinction has arisen from theoretical shortcomings such as limiting linguistics and semantics more or less to the denotative aspects of talking (and writing), then a more general conception of signs and semiotics is required to analyze the connotative senses of speech, the different levels of interpretation involving context, as well as all the other forms of communication. This study is meant as a contribution in that direction. There is no sense studying the implicit without the explicit, the non-verbal without the verbal, silence without talk, since they are all parts of a whole, and are complementary, not contradictory.

In the foregoing chapter we saw how storytelling was often clouded with uncertainty as to the origin of the knowledge revealed, and how some stories were left unmentioned in certain cases. This foreshadowed the functioning of the general quest for silence and discretion to be examined here. But precaution as applied to talking has not only to do with telling stories, it is present in all communication, and is both implicitly and explicitly expressed. Implicitly, it is expressed in the preference for speaking indirectly, with few words or none at all. Explicitly, the principles of silence, discretion and indiscretion are often evoked through expressions *about* talking.

Explicit Principles

Silence is not only exercised, it is often talked about, which is of course a contrast to the fundamentals of silence itself. The following expressions are often used to characterize others. But while talking about others, people often make overt, reflexive comments on their own talking.

— *trop causer:*
A very common and negative charge to make about someone is to say *"il cause trop"* (literally, he talks too much).[2] But this generally means the person talks too openly rather than abundantly. Here, we already see that the relationship between talking and silence is judged relatively according to circumstance, i.e., according to the sliding scale between public and private. Talking in private, however loquaciously, is rarely characterized as *"trop,"* whereas talking in public can easily be. Hence, the assessment of what is too much is relative, not definite or absolute, since the border between private and public is itself just as vague; and conversely, the degree of privateness/publicness of a context is determined precisely by factors like the ease of the flow of conversation.

The classical example of someone who according to local standards *causait trop* was a local drunkard who was not afraid of insulting people and saying in public what everyone else only said in private. Furthermore, he was usually quite well informed about what went on in the community. The attitude towards him was quite ambiguous: people both resented and enjoyed his directness, and sometimes even relied on him for spreading news, as in the story of the emptied mill-pond (Chapter 2.2). On several occasions during my stay, he publicly insulted other villagers, especially the instigators of the land reallotment, which in those days was a delicate matter and the biggest source of tension between neighbours. Those who concurred with him in private were of course delighted by his public performance, although they would never show this, and everyone kept him at a safe distance so as not to be directly, publicly associated with his exclamations.

To my ears, what he said was quite harmless, like "you pickle" (*espèce de cornichon*) and "townhall nobody's" (*nuls de mairie*). But to others it wasn't, and the face-to-face directness and yelling certainly offended and frightened them just as much as the content. This did not prevent people from associating with him privately, though: he was known to everyone as a regular conversationalist and cardplayer at the "against" (-reallotment) bistro. Somehow, he was only dangerous in

---

2 *"Causer"* is usually translated as "to chatter," but in the present context it is used alternately with *"parler,"* "to speak." Generally, *"il parle trop"* (he talks too much) is used in very much the same way as *"il cause trop."*

public, and as a result always appeared unaccompanied.3 Socializing with him elsewhere did not seem to compromise others, it did not reflect on them, probably because he was completely predictable and never broke his word, and when he did yell, it was still in quite a controlled way: he never said anything untrue, and never gave his allies away. I was referred to him several times when I asked questions about, for example, witchcraft cases – not so much because people believed he might satisfy my curiosity, but as a way of telling me that only he would know the answers to such bothersome questions; that he, unlike others, probably wouldn't mind telling me the answers; and mainly, that I was asking too much, since I could only expect a fool drunkard to answer.

In connection with the land reallotment, there was a warning about people who did not respect the "for" and "against" groupings and talked to members of both camps: "Watch your step, he talks too much" (*Faut se méfier, il cause trop*). This meant the person might go over and repeat everything he heard to people in the other faction. It also meant his information was unreliable since he was obviously saying one thing in one group and something else in the other in order to agree with everyone. Talking too much with a person like that was avoided – to protect information of course, but also as though his unreliability were contagious.

"*Il cause trop*" was also said in another tone of persons who boasted of, for example, removing the surveyors' landmarks, in this case because they were endangering themselves. It was thought such imprudence might land them in jail, but it also compromised those who were told. In one case, a person reacted quite violently to such boasting, saying angrily: "Shut up, you talk too much!" (*Tais-toi, tu causes trop!*) Although he already knew about the affair, he would have preferred not to be told directly in front of witnesses, thus openly party to information he could be suspected of leaking.

---

3 This re-confirms that the relationship between private and public is relative, comprising contextually defined spaces rather than clearly designated places: the bistro can be considered both a public and private space according to who inhabits it and what the relations are between these persons.

– *bien causer:*
This expression can be understood two different ways: quantitatively, as meaning "to talk a lot" (and hence, "too much"); and qualitatively, "to speak well," indicating that a person is a talented speaker with a good mastery of the French language. A person referred to the first way excels within the local sphere of discourse but talks too much, whereas referred to the second way, he or she speaks quite another and more official language. In using the expression in the first sense, the speaker distances himself from the object of his observation, someone who does not control their flow of words well enough, whereas in the second sense, a distance already in place is commented upon. People, who "speak well" (*parlent bien*) in the sense of mastering a different order of discourse, are dealt with cautiously. Whether they come from the outside, like civil servants and the Mayor, or are locals who received higher education, they are thought to be evoking social difference on purpose, to be condescending to villagers, and furthermore, to have administrative powers that could impinge upon and be dangerous to the everyday life of people in the village. Those with good diction represent the faraway and omnipotent central administration (often both symbolically and in actuality).

On the other hand, saying of someone that *"elle cause pas bien"* (she doesn't speak well) might actually be compliment, meaning the person is reserved and does not talk *much*.

– *pipelet(te), bavard(e):*
These are quite common words in French, meaning gossipy and talkative. Such words are used to describe others in much the same way as above, but also to refer to oneself. People often apologized for being *pipelet* or *bavard*, even when we were alone. "*Qu'est-ce-qu'on est bavard, hein?*" – We're such talkers, aren't we? "*On parle, hein, on papote.*" – We sure can talk, eh, just gabbing. Like the expression *"faut pas l'dire,"* such excusing was done periodically during conversation, as if to remind us we were on touchy ground, to say something about the situation under discussion and about the intimacy, even conspiracy, shared by the persons talking.

– *flatteur/euse:*
If *pipelet* and *bavard* were not always used negatively, *"flatteur/euse"* (flatterer) is on the contrary very negatively charged, implying that the person in question not only flatters but arbitrarily echoes whomever he or she is talking with, regardless of groupings. The person is a traitor and a hypocrite, unreliable because never sincere to anyone, never really choosing sides. *"Oh, celui-la, il est flatteur. Il parle comme celui qui lui paye le canon."* – He's a *flatteur*. He goes along with whoever's buying the drinks. *"Elle est flatteuse. Il faut toujours entendre le contraire de ce qu'elle dit."* – She's *flatteuse*. Always believe the opposite of what she says. *"Faut s'méfier, hein. Un jour ils disent une chose, l'autre ils disent le contraire."* – Watch out. They say one thing one day and another the next.

On the other hand, an expression that means one keeps one's word and does not go indiscriminately from camp to camp is: *"J'ai pas trente-six paroles."*

Taking an active part in social life almost always implies choosing sides. But another option is living in retreat, not participating, and thus not having allies. People who choose this are completely outside of social life. *"Ils sont dans le néant"* – they're in the void – was said of a local couple. This is seen as regrettable, but not reproachable. A third option is participating in social life without taking sides, constantly going from one to the other. This is viewed as inadvisable.

– *names:*
A common name in the region is Parlebas, which, according to how it is divided, is directly translated as either "by the low (road)" (*par le bas*) or "speak low" (lower your voice: *parle bas*). It might be somewhat exaggerated to call this an explicit expression of the quest for discretion and silence, but names in the region often have quite worldly origins and the latter interpretation makes more sense than the first.

I am not saying that the expressions and words I have described here are unique to the region. I do claim, though, that they are very regularly used, that in almost every conversation talking is talked about, and that in every opinion expressed about someone else, reference is made to the person's handling of verbal communication.

Implicit Principles

Indirect Speech

A very common way of safely and discreetly expressing oneself is by doing it indirectly, articulating a few very suggestive words, saying something else that will surely be interpreted the right way, or saying it with no words at all, using other signs. As we have seen in the incident of the emptied millpond (Chapter 2), it is also possible to have one's words disseminated by others. It is obvious, though, that what I consider indirect speech is for local people perfectly clear and direct.

We have already seen many examples of ways of being discreet yet clear; the stories were full of such examples. Here I will just mention a few more.

– saying Few Suggestive Words:

When a person is expressing a point of view – his appreciation for or dislike of another person, for example – to someone whose opinion he is unsure of, the speaker's first approach is usually very imprecise and ambiguous, not even a clear point of view, enabling him to pull out at any moment without giving himself away. If the standpoint seems to be mutual, the interlocutors slowly approach an expressed common opinion, giving convincing examples of the conduct of the subject of their conversation, and mutually confirming one another in the process.

In general, because everybody knows everything, it is quite easy to say things with few words and always be understood. Most people recognize this way of mutual understanding from their close relationships. In La Brumaire, however, the phenomenon is extended to the whole community. To an outsider, words are coded and their sense determined by context; to an insider, they are perfectly clear and denotative.[4]

---

4 Being somewhere between the two, I instantly got the message in some cases without thinking about it; in others, I didn't even notice there was one because I had not understood. In yet other cases, I was bewildered, aware that there was a message, and that I hadn't caught it. In any case, working without sound-recording made it difficult to recapture previously unnoticed messages, and thus to present them here. What I did catch was what made sense at the moment and with the level of understanding I had obtained.

A typical example is when, after the usual introductory salutations, like "*Ça va-t'y?*" (How are you?), and a pause, someone asks: "*Alors?*" (So?...) with a sly look on their face. Puzzled in the beginning by the vagueness of a question that obviously demanded a clear answer, I soon came to understand that it had an exact meaning in every case. "*Alors?*" always referred to the occurrence of very specific events and a tense situation, and meant: "Did you know? So what do you think of it?" As one might imagine, the answers were equally vague and indirect.

– saying Something Else:
Using few or other words altogether does not make a big difference, except that other words are perhaps clearer to the stranger witnessing an exchange of surprisingly divergent sentences. In other cases, the stranger's own innocent words are interpreted according to local rules. I once asked if houses were often for sale in the area, and everyone present immediately understood that I wanted to buy a house in the village, although I was not thinking that far ahead. I was speaking the same way they do. Without talking about myself or my personal plans, I had made myself perfectly clear, although my primary intent was to know if people were leaving the region. But knowing the context of my living- and working situation, people anticipated my intentions. Intentionally "masking" one's words is another matter; this I only mastered after quite a long time in the village.

A man had inherited a neighbour's land and farm, as well as her many cats. Some people were inclined to think he had been too lucky and did not deserve the inheritance – he actually bought it, but at a rather low price. As for the cats, no one else wanted them, although they didn't seem to bother him. As a way of letting him know he had unrightfully inherited, people would say to him, "You can always do away with the cats, of course." This was not just friendly advice, it meant something like: "Now that she's dead, you can admit they are a nuisance you put up with just to get your hands on her assets." On the other hand, to assure us of his gratitude and good intentions, he told us furiously several times how he had responded by throwing the cat-offenders out of his house with the retort, "As if you're not allowed to like cats."

A farmer had an unfaithful wife. His friends said, "If he throws her out, he'll have to sell the farm and give her half." This implied that he knew about her infidelity and that, but for the fact that he was concerned about his farm, he surely would have reacted that way, thrown her out, like a man. The local importance and respect assigned to land were his alibi, saved his honour and wore down his horns.

– speaking Through Others:
We have already seen how people rely on others to spread their messages and be their unofficial spokesperson, like the village drunkard, for example, when he insulted supporters of the land reallotment. This is quite a widespread mechanism.

In other cases, communication is more targeted but still passes through an intermediary. Marriage proposals passed through an official intermediary until recently, for instance. Occasionally people mentioned who went as the intermediary to ask for a bride's hand when they were speaking about the elders of the village. La Salle also describes this institution, calling the intermediary *"le menon"* (1902: 48).

More common today is the strategic messenger, asked by someone to intervene in case of a problem or conflict. This strategy was employed several times during my stay, in connection with smaller conflicts between allies – about land, machines, unreturned favours, etc. This was obviously also the role assigned to my mother-in-law when she was asked to be Association Secretary and represent the landowners to the administration during the land reallotment. She was also often authorized to represent individual landowners who did not dare present themselves in person: *"Je n' voudrais pas m' montrer, mais comme c'est important..."* (I don't want to show myself, but since it's important...). The fact that they preferred to avoid direct confrontation was perfectly acceptable, even considered wise.

The avoidance of saying things directly and of employing precise unequivocal words is prevalent. Although all statements between Brumairians are always clearly understood and thus in some way precise, they are nevertheless shrouded in a mist of ambiguity and inaccuracy that makes retreat possible if necessary. Statements remain reversible. This is another aspect of the paradox of silence and talk. Let us recall the example of a person who is bothered by being told something clearly and directly by a reliable source. He already knew the information, perhaps through someone else, by having seen something, or just by knowing the person in question, and he was already satisfied with his knowledge and comfortable with its degree of uncertainty.

Finally, a remark about the use of telephones: although almost everyone has a telephone, they clearly prefer to deliver their messages in person, even if they have to travel five kilometres or more to do so. If they use the phone, the conversation is always pared down to the bare necessities. This shows of course a very positive preference for direct human contact, but it is mainly a clear avoidance of the telephone. Only words (and their delimiting silences) come through on the phone, all other ways of communicating are excluded, and words must compensate for this by being all the more direct. That is probably why people prefer face-to-face contact. Telephoning has other aspects, which we will come back to in the next chapter: it is, in a certain way, a negation of doing, of public action. By telephoning, one fails to inscribe a social message in the landscape with one's movement through it.

Discretion

Pursuant to earlier remarks I made about discretion in general, I will go on here to discuss the principles of discretion at work when two or more persons are talking together in private, whether at home, in the fields, at the bistro or any other place where people are liable to meet:

– *speaking in an Undertone:*
When important information is being handled, voices are automatically lowered. This is both a message about the character of what is about to be said, and a security measure.

– *moving Toward One Another:*
The lowering of voices is accompanied by a slight shifting of chairs and/or bending of heads together to close the circle.

– *environmental Glance:*
The last security measure, whether in the bistro, a stable or in the confines of a private kitchen, is everyone taking a rapid glance around at

the surroundings. Ostensibly, no place is completely safe against eavesdropping intruders, let alone distant but observant onlookers. During the conversation, eyes continue to glance around, checking movements and changes in the vicinity.

These measures are, of course, part of a whole discursive and social *mise en scène*, as we saw earlier. They codify the participants as confidants and the information as confidential, such codification in itself acting as a discretional measure. But such measures are also very concrete and important means of assuring security, meant to avoid direct leakage. Furthermore, conversation takes a form such that, should an intruder enter hearing range, the flow of information can stop at once with no obvious breach. A person who suddenly entered the bistro would have no idea that important knowledge had been passed on just five seconds earlier, let alone what subject of it might be. This precaution is achieved through short, condensed sentences punctuated with pauses and casual neutral remarks. Should someone interrupt a conversation, all he would hear would be, *"Eh, ben, oui!"* – Well, well... (I quickly learned that saying *"Ah bon?"* (Really?) and *"Ça, alors!"* (No kidding!) were seriously overstated and extremely indiscreet responses in conversation.) This pattern bears no relationship to ingenuousness of a continuous flow of words, halted abruptly mid-sentence and followed by throat-clearing and blushing, such as one might encounter walking into a highschool locker-room unannounced. In the social sphere of La Brumaire, discourse is all perfectly controlled.

Not-Hearing

The most current examples I have of people consciously ignoring what others say as a discretional measure concern myself and the village drunkard, two persons who did not always say the right thing at the right moment. I have already mentioned his unbecoming yelling and verbal assaults which people tried to ignore. In my case, ignoring was always done in connection with my questioning something. At first, if I got no reaction, I would repeat the question and be, at best, met with an annoyed glance, if anything. Eventually, it became quite clear: I asked "too much," or rather, with questions that were not part of a normal exchange of words and information, I should not expect an answer. I quickly discovered that anything I ever learned about questioning and interviewing techniques was not only useless but should be avoided. In general, people did not ask precise questions, and only completely open incitements like "*Ça va-t'y?*" (How's it going?) "*Quoi de neuf?*" (What's new?) or "*Alors?*" (So?...) were acceptable. More precise questions would be an expression of overt curiosity, revealing the questioner's knowledge too directly, and would put the person questioned in the awkward position of being forced to answer. One old woman in the village was clearly shunned because she always asked too many questions: "*Y faut s'en méfier, hein! Elle pose trop d' questions*" (Watch out for her, she asks too many questions).

People knew very well I was conducting a study, but that did not entitle me to neglect local standards of conversational exchange. Only when my questions clearly dealt with the land reallotment – an exceptional situation requiring appropriate, out-of-the-ordinary responses – were they honoured with answers. The point of asking was clear, and the interest in answering obvious. The threat of losing land was in itself a provocation that demanded a response, any question about it on my part was only a point of mediation. In this case, answering was not "saying too much to a stranger" (giving something away), but defending oneself (returning something), and thus maintaining the essence of exchange.

Not-hearing is part of the general principle of silence: by not-hearing, people indirectly request the unfortunate speaker's silence, and express their own wish to keep silent on a matter at the same time.

Simulating Ignorance

Like not-hearing, simulating ignorance is also part of the general quest for silence, and a very common way of keeping quiet. It is also a way to tell another to stop asking. And finally, it is a way of showing that one does not know everything. In the beginning, I was quite surprised when people said "I don't know" to fairly inoffensive questions they obviously could answer, like "Is your father working in the fields today?" But I eventually learned not to take the answer at face value, but as a comment on my inquisitiveness – something like, "That's none of your business today."

Simulating ignorance in discussions about current village affairs is also quite common. It is a way to make the other tell more, but it is also a way of stressing that one has better things to do than pry into what's going on in the village – which of course is never true. I experienced this pattern directly when people feigned not knowing who I was or that we were making a film. (I was probably the only tall blonde with a strange accent within seventy-five kilometres, and awareness of the film spread before we even took out the camera).

Of course, feigning ignorance is a common way of expressing oneself in most parts of the world, but that does not make it any less worthy of describing in detail. And feigning ignorance as I experienced it in La Brumaire was much more persistent than anywhere else. This holds true of all the phenomena described here. They are more than just ways, they are phenomena, and together, seem to constitute a whole "culture of silence".

Lying

Lying is very strongly resented. Silence, or claiming not to know something – i.e., deliberately withholding – is, however, not considered lying, it is thought of as discretion. Expressly saying something false is not being discreet.

In the story of the stolen jacket, the main offense (and the reason it became a story) was that the person who took the jacket also claimed he never saw it. Had he simply taken it, the owner could have asked to have it back, but since the thief lied, the other man chose to leave and not openly reveal the offense. The breach of communication superseded the theft, as in "The Child in the Dunghill," where the dissemination of knowledge through odour superseded the infanticide.

A man once asked me if he could cross our courtyard, which gives onto a brook, making a great fuss out of unfolding his fishing-rods. Rivers are public, and people have the right to fish from anyone's land. Later, when a neighbour saw his car leaving, I explained he had been fishing. "*Ha, ha, ha, il n'a jamais su pêcher, lui ! Il a été chercher des escargots. Il vous a eu, là*" (Ha, ha, he's never known how to fish. He was picking snails. He got you there). Unlike fish, snails are private, not public property. But the man wasn't exactly lying, since he was careful not to say he was going fishing.

A woman rented some land from a neighbour, but then let someone else use it for his horses. When called on the matter, she said the horse-owner was only paying for the hay and not for renting the land, which would be a violation of her lease. This was a way of diverting the issue, of course. When asked directly if he wasn't paying her a little under the table, she didn't answer. Our neighbour knows the horse-owner, and thus knows the woman did not want to risk being caught in a lie, so she chose to keep silent.

Quite a lot of lying has gone on in connection with the land reallotment, mainly by the Mayor, known as a *"rapporté"* ("brought in," someone who moved to the village from elsewhere), and by the executing surveyors, also non-villagers. Lies have mainly been about judicial procedure and economic questions: e.g., stating that geological tests would be conducted before any work was undertaken (subsequently proven false); convincing people that they can refuse the "proposed exchanges" (completely false: they are simply expropriated); saying they don't have to pay for eventual differences in amounts of land (also false); asserting that such differences in size between original properties and re-mapped ones will not legally exceed two to three percent of the person's acreage included in the reallotment, when the actual figure is ten percent.[5] This means a person could end up with an area smaller than he had before, but if the opposite is the case, he has to pay for extra land he has not even asked for. In the extreme case, this could represent a cost of around 50.000 francs, more than a year's income for many people.

Everyone assumes that those involved in executing the land reallotment are more or less dishonest, but no one will believe that they are actually lying. For instance, a person found it very difficult to believe that the Mayor could have been lying to him about the aforementioned percentages. When he was finally convinced by seeing an extract of the law, he was extremely shocked, not so much by the information itself as by the fact that the Mayor deliberately lied to him. Mainly, the man felt very humiliated. Furthermore, having believed the Mayor, the man had probably repeated the lie to others, which in turn made him a liar. He had been contaminated.

---

5 To simplify, I speak of surface area, but it is actually a point system, where points are attributed according to the surface area and quality of the land.

Most of the lies surrounding the reallotment have been quite technical, belonging to a different, "outside" order of discourse, and profiting from that fact (e.g., assuming that no local would think of checking the relevant laws). However, there have also been some lies about people in the village, thus inside the order of local discourse and control – for example, saying certain persons were for the reallotment when they were actually against, and assuring unsure persons that their neighbours were willing to exchange certain fields when they were not. The list of lies and manipulations is unfortunately much too long to be completely enumerated here.

Lying imposes itself on the innocent receiver and can be contagious. Giving no information, silence, respects the person to whom one is (not) talking, whereas giving false information, lying, takes things out of their control, making it extremely dangerous.

Silence

Again, according to the way I deal with it here, silence is communicative, meaningful and implies knowing. Within this definition there are different forms of silence. There are what I call "generalized silences" – specific subjects that everyone avoids talking about. There are more circumstantial silences contingent on where, why, and who is involved. Finally, there are "real silences" that exist outside the domain of communication. In many cases, silence is expressed by "I don't know" (*je n' sais pas*), simulated ignorance. In others, there is just silence, with no excuse. In either case, silence is a response to someone else's expectations, otherwise it makes no sense.

– generalized Silences:
Generalized silences could be likened to taboos; as defined by a villager: "*On n'parle pas d'ça ici !* (We don't talk about that here!)

One thing people stringently avoid talking about is their deceased relatives, especially if they were close family members: husbands, wives, parents and children. Even close friends and neighbours are talked about with caution. If a subject is unavoidable, a practical matter, voices are lowered and the discussion concluded as quickly as possible. If I talked about someone who was dead, people answered with vague mumbling, visibly troubled. During my two-year stay, two close friends of mine, a father and son, mentioned their wife/mother (who had died four years earlier) on only one occasion and with low voices, to explain how they got a certain field from her side of the family. Likewise, several sons avoided talking about their respective fathers. One old woman, after praising a deceased woman for having been a good housewife – "Not once in all those years did they come home from the fields without her having lunch ready, not once." – explicity said of her widower: "I don't talk to George about her any more now that she's dead" (*Georges, je n'lui parle pas d'elle, c'est pas la peine d'en parler, qu'elle est morte*). And finally, no one ever asked about my father-in-law who, unlike my mother-in-law, had family roots in the region, although they obviously would have liked to know something about him. But the taboo was stronger than their curiosity.

Another subject that is generally avoided is talking concretely about one's income and resources. Exact figures of people's incomes were something I never heard discussed, and the size of people's farms was always only roughly estimated by others and never really elucidated by the owners. In connection with the land reallotment, such figures had to be revealed to the Association, and this was done with only slight reservation, both because the reason was practical and self-protective, and because figures for rented land did not appear, thus still concealing the real worth of people's resources. On one occasion, I helped some farmers fill in a form so that they could be indemnified for a period of drought, making note of the grain in their fields and in the ones they were renting. This opened up very intimate knowledge and the situation was consequently very intense, with lowered voices and eyes fixed on the papers and on each other. I was already quite intimate with the persons in question, but afterwards I became even closer, and was let in on other intimate details, and once even shown a photo of a deceased relative. Making me more party to the private sanctum also made me less liable to talk about what I knew.

People generally avoid talking about themselves with the exception of talking about their illnesses. I must say, never in my life, not even as a hospital orderly, have I heard such detailed descriptions of stomach diseases, kidney problems, cancer symptoms, operations, medications and cures. This is in sharp contrast to the tacit avoidance of self-reference. Part of the explanation could be that illness is seen as caused by exterior factors. One is not a responsible, active agent in disease; one only suffers passively while the illness takes action. Talking about illness is thus talking about someone or something other than oneself. Only when illness is conceived within the discourse of witchcraft, where the factors are social (jealous neighbours and relatives), does silence prevail. The factors causing illness are generally unknown and do not belong to the social field, which brings talking about illness into the domain of "rumour" as defined above: there is one-way influence but no relationship.

Real Silence

Finally, there is the domain of real silence. Even when people avoid making sound, I still say their silence talks. But a domain of complete and unassailable silence remains. There are things that are just not talked about, with or without words. Respect for the individual leaves this area inviolable, unviolated and even uninterpreted, both in general and in my analysis.

In the beginning of my fieldwork, I often had the impression I was touching upon areas people wanted left alone. But as time went by, I was increasingly admitted into what I had thought untouchable, and I realized how relative (and relational) silence and privacy are.

Yet at a certain point I had to acknowledge there were things remaining that were never discussed. Some of them I could conceptualize and understand – like not mentioning the dead or not talking about sorcery – precisely because there were a few exceptions to the rule, making the hidden conceivable. But other things never came to the surface, they remained perfectly hidden to me. I came to think that there existed a mode unlike other forms of information, unlike the stories, constantly stating, transgressing and erasing the borderline between private and public – a domain of real silence, signifying and delimiting a true and unnegotiable private realm that cannot be violated. I could only see the limit and what was outside it, and there was no reason to try and guess what is on the other side. Suffice it to say, there is something and it will be respected.

If this domain of profound silence betrayed nothing of its own content, it said something about my ideas: if the really private does exist, it brings the principle of complementarity to its own inherent extreme by proving that private-public is not only "both-and," but *both* both/and, *and* either/or. The "private" at the extreme end of the private-public scale is real enough; it is not just a relative concept. It *is* purely private.

3.2 The Power of Words

The fact that words are subject to discretional measures and even silence definitely has something to do with the influence and control words exert over people's lives. Words are powerful instruments in defining and negotiating the identity of one's neighbours and oneself. We have seen this both in stories and in the modes of silence, and we can see it in the following display of magical discourses about others, and in what I have called "parallel discourses."

When I first came to La Brumaire, I had been immersed for some time in Jeanne Favret-Saada's writings about witchcraft in the southern Norman Bocage, an area about 200 kilometres northwest of the region I was visiting. Not only was her work fabulous reading, but I was intrigued by the parallels I found between her descriptions and what I encountered in La Brumaire, just as much on general economic and social grounds as in the field of communication and day-to-day relations between people. It occurred to me that what she called the "discourse of witchcraft," a discourse which lay at the centre of her work, could perhaps be included in the more general category, "talking about neighbours," because, although I didn't immediately run into discourses about witchcraft, what I did encounter was a whole range of discourses about others. The people I met were basically saying the same things as Favret-Saada's interlocutors about the influence neighbours had on each other's existence, but without employing the symbolics of magic and supernatural forces.

It also occurred to me that if I couldn't really get a handle on silences and their meanings, there certainly had to be a relationship – perhaps one of complementarity – between the power of words and silence. It is not the case that people simply kept silent because words were too strong (such case would furnish a simple "explanation of the phenomenon of silence"), but that *both* words and silence were strong discursive instruments, exchanged with equal importance and significance in defining others and oneself.

Witchcraft in the Norman Bocage
There are two completely entwined sides of Favret-Saada's work that demand attention: her descriptions of Bocage witchcraft and her praxis as a highly engaged fieldworker.

Favret-Saada originally came to the Bocage of southern Normandy with the intention of studying "the practices of sorcery" (*les pratiques de sorcellerie*), that is, how people there performed witchcraft (Favret-Saada 1977: 25). But she soon found out there *were* no sorcerers; there were only people bewitched, and "unwitchers."[6]

The only empirical facts she ever encountered stemmed from people talking about sorcery and sorcerers, perceiving themselves as victims of sorcerers and counteracting their spells through "unwitching." Of course, certain unlucky persons were sometimes pointed out as sorcerers by presumed victims and/or unwitchers, but nothing ever indicated to Favret-Saada that any supposed sorcerer had actually taken action.

> The witch is the person referred to by those who utter the discourse on witchcraft (bewitched and unwitchers), and he only figures in it as the subject of the statement...But that did not seem to disturb the actual functioning of the system of bewitchment. (1980: 24)[7]

In short, what she met in the Bocage was the discourse of witchcraft, between supposed victims and their unwitchers (1971: 335; 1986: 30).

Although Favret-Saada could not deal with sorcery as an actual offensive praxis, the symbolic system of defensive discourse that she met through persons talking about witchcraft perfectly outlined the mechanisms of sorcery:

A person who is jealous of someone else can cast a spell by pronouncing certain malefic words found in books like *Le Petit Albert* or *Le Grand Albert*. It is always the head of a farm who is bewitched, although he or she can be reached through other members of the household, through livestock or through material equipment, thereby draining all capacity to produce and reproduce, all vital force (1989: 43).

Invariably, the sorcerer is someone who is jealous of another person's luck and wealth. He or she never resides within the household, considered an economic and moral entity. The sorcerer can be someone who

---

6 Selected terms and citations are from Favret-Saada 1980 (which is the English edition of Favret-Saada 1977). Other translations are mine.

7 "*Le sorcier, c'est l'être dont parlent ceux qui tiennent le discours de la sorcellerie (ensorcelés et désenvoûteurs) et il n'apparaît que comme sujet de l'énoncé. ... Cela rend très improbable qu'il existe quelque sorcier qui pratiquerait effectivement des maléfices, mais on se doute que cela n'est pas du tout nécessaire au fonctionnement du système*" (1977: 50).

feels cheated in connection with an inheritance, hence a relative, or a neighbour who is just generally envious. Thus, the sorcerer is always someone close, but not too close.

Sorcerers' spells result in a whole variety of lesser evils for the bewitched, beginning with, for example, white mushrooms appearing in the fields and cows no longer giving milk, strange sounds in empty rooms and small accidents, and eventually leading to more serious accidents, illnesses, sterility, madness, dwindling livestock and even people's deaths.

As individual occurrences, such events are never interpreted as signs of witchcraft, but with repetition, such an interpretation becomes justified, leading to the open denunciation of sorcery and the summoning of a *"désorceleur,"* an unwitcher. The unwitcher in turn arranges a whole series of retaliatory rituals and measures, constituted mainly of counter-spells and formulas to be pronounced by both the unwitcher and the bewitched person. Evil forces are thereby turned back on the sorcerer, and eventually result in his or her misfortune, illness and eventual death. Even if the unwitcher has been unable to name a sorcerer, his or her identity is nevertheless ultimately revealed through the incidents of bad luck that strike him or her in return.

> His victims claim that it is unnecessary for him to admit he is a witch, since his death speaks for him: everyone laughs at his funeral because he died in a significant way, carried off in only a few hours as a result of the diviner's curse, or neighing like the mare he had cast an evil spell on, and so on. (Favret-Saada 1980: 24)[8]

– You just have to take a look around the village to know.

The precautions to be taken by bewitched persons can be characterized as forms of closure. In concrete terms, bewitched persons "must close everything up" (*il faut tout clencher*): they must shut doors, windows and gates, denying the sorcerer open access to their physical person, as well as to their cohabitants and belongings. The bewitched must close their mouth in his presence, they must "shut" their body, never

---

8 *"Ses victimes assurent qu'il n'a pas besoin de s'avouer sorcier, parce que sa mort parle pour lui: chacun rit à ses funérailles parce qu'il est mort de façon significative, emporté en quelques heures à la suite d'une prédiction d'un devin ou bien en hennissant comme la jument qu'il maléficiait, etc."* (1977: 50).

touch him, never shake his hand. Such physical barriers are reinforced by magic barriers: religious medallions, holy water and salt are placed or sprinkled everywhere, and places or things that move or that cannot be physically locked up or enclosed, like fields, cars and free-ranging animals, are "shut up" by encircling them with salt or holy water (1986: 33-34).

These general mechanisms of sorcery and its treatment in the Norman Bocage are described by Favret-Saada in *Les mots, la mort, les sorts* (1977) as well as *Corps pour corps* (Favret-Saada & Contreras 1981) (a selection of her fieldnotes dating from July, 1969, to December, 1970), and in a series of articles (Favret-Saada 1971, 1986, 1987, 1989).

Apart from the silent figure of the sorcerer, whom Favret-Saada never had occasion to hear, there are three main types of interlocutors involved in the discourses of sorcery: the "annunciator" (*annonciateur*), the person bewitched and the unwitcher. The annunciator identifies the mishaps striking a person (and/or his or her household) as signs of sorcery, and thus determines this person as being bewitched. Before such an assessment, the unhappy household appeared to be merely suffering from a number of apparently unlinked accidents and problems they were unable to associate and explain, let alone deal with. But with the pronouncement, "there may be someone who wants to do you harm" (*Il y a peut-être quelqu'un qui vous veut du mal*), the afflicted enter into the previously unknown reign of witchcraft, and are vested by the unwitcher with instruments to deal with and divert their misfortune. Both the reign of witchcraft and most of the retaliatory instruments are constituted primarily of words. Sorcery – that is, being bewitched and unwitching – is discourse.

But how can the annunciator determine that the misery of a family is due to sorcery when the family itself had not the slightest idea? The answer to this has to do with another crucial concept, *"d'être pris"* (to be taken in or caught). For, contrary to common ideas about witchcraft, sorcery in this specific cultural and temporal context is not a widespread cultural phenomenon: it is very restricted and has clear limits. *"D'être pris"* implies that a person has abandoned the dominant rational belief that witchcraft and maledictions are backward and superstitious, and has acknowledged through personal experience that sorcery is a valid explanation for an otherwise irrational situation. *"D'être pris"* means believing in sorcery from having suffered it. "'For those who haven't been caught, they [spells] don't exist,'" and furthermore, "'Those who haven't been caught can't even talk about it'" (1980: 15).9 They cannot even conceive of it. The annunciator is typically someone who has him- or herself been bewitched, whereas the suffering family had never before given it serious thought.

This brings up another important side to Favret-Saada's work: how she herself entered the regime of witchcraft and came to "know." When she arrived in the Bocage as an acknowledged Parisian scientist interested in studying local forms of witchcraft, people were disinclined to think she actually believed in it, so they talked to her about their problems accordingly – on an official and rational basis, pretending to have heard of spells only indirectly or from a distance, and declaring witchcraft to be "'superstitions of backward people,'" "'beliefs of the old folk'" (ibid.: 15-16). That is how one talks to someone who is supposedly not "*pris*."

Those who know about witchcraft have had personal experience with it, and the only acceptable reasons for talking to a stranger about the personal experience of witchcraft would be: 1) to give an account of one's situation to someone capable of changing it, that is, to an unwitcher; 2) to speak of one's own experiences so as to alert someone else to witchcraft, that is, take on the role of annunciator for a person presumably bewitched; 3) to be an unwitcher talking to a bewitched client. In any case, the respective positions are clear.

"To talk, in witchcraft, is never to inform. Or if information is given, it is so that the person who is to kill (the unwitcher) will know where to aim his blows" (1980: 9).10 Just as it was impossible that anyone might talk to Favret-Saada about witchcraft for no other reason than to inform her, it was inconceivable that she would ask about witchcraft just for the sake of knowing, to develop her scientific work. As a result, she came to "know" only when one of the aforementioned roles was attributed to her by her interlocutors when, without initially noticing, she

---

9 "*Pour ceux qui n'ont pas été pris, ça n'existe pas.*" "*Ceux qui n'ont pas été pris, ils ne peuvent pas en parler*" (1977: 35).
10 "*Parler en sorcellerie, c'est jamais pour informer. Ou si l'on informe, c'est pour que celui qui doit tuer (le désenvoûteur) sache où faire porter ses coups*" (1977: 26).

was (mis)taken for an unwitcher by a family in distress, and later, when a series of mishaps that befell her was interpreted as the result of witchcraft. "As with any other interlocutor, speaking to the ethnographer one is addressing *a subject supposed to be able* (a witch, an unwitcher) *or unable* (a victim, a bewitched person)" (1980: 11).[11] In both cases, as unwitcher and as victim, she was definitely involved, if not to say completely absorbed.

To sum up, witchcraft is first and foremost a discourse, a *relational* discourse, about others and about one's relationship to them. Bad luck is not an internal matter, but an external one. The patterned misfortune that betrays witchcraft is due to relations of inequality, one's bad luck being the result of someone else's jealousy. The discourse of witchcraft articulates an impression of imbalance in a social and economic situation, an imbalance which the jealous sorcerer tries to tip to his advantage. His weapons are words, his power stems from magic formulas obtained in books that are accessible to anyone. With these words he can exert influence upon and control the life of a fellow villager.

Witchcraft in Le Berry
As I mentioned, it took quite a while before I was let in on even the slightest details about what could be designated "sorcery" in La Brumaire. Sorcery was obviously part of a very private sphere of discourse, and was subject to rather categorical silence. When I was eventually admitted into such spheres of intimacy, it was clearly for a reason, and because in various situations I could be qualified as something close to *"prise."*

I was not looking for stories about witchcraft over other kinds of stories, and with Favret-Saada's work in mind, I was quite prudent. I did not want to be taken for someone I was not. Furthermore, I did not proceed from the assumption that entering people's private spheres was reaching an ultimate goal, an innermost part of communal life. Like silence, there were boundaries to be respected. For my purposes, noticing

---

11 "*Comme à n'importe quel locuteur, c'est à un* sujet supposé pouvoir *(un sorcier, un désenvoûteur)* ou ne pas pouvoir *(une victime, un ensorcelé) qu'on s'adresse lorsqu'on parle à l'ethnographe*" (1977: 29).

my interlocutors draw these boundaries was just as important and interesting as seeing them erased.

As for Favret-Saada, *time* came to play an important role here, allowing my position to evolve, and encouraging people to open up to secrets that had earlier been shrouded in silence. Observing these changes was valuable. Had there been no reluctance in the beginning, no silence, transformed over the course of events into discreet openness, there would have been no "object." What made it a phenomenon was the relativity – the transgression and continual transformation of relations. And I too was an object of observation, my own guinea pig, so to speak, as I registered my own access to knowledge.

Of course it was uncertain whether phenomena like those described by Favret-Saada could also be found in the area of La Brumaire, but it was probable. Quite a lot of popular literature, fiction, and semi-scientific books and articles have been written on the subject, and even quite recently, affairs involving sorcery have been described in the local press. The tone of such literature is always either ridiculing, treating the local population as backward and superstitious, or pop-traditionalist with a touch of paternalism, describing Le Berry, and especially the Boischaut Sud where La Brumaire is situated, as a kind of undeveloped island "deep" in France (*la France profonde*), where pagan traditions have survived through the centuries despite the evolution of the surrounding world. In the latter category of material, the fruit of Jean-Louis Boncoeur's industry (books, records, postcards, etc.) is quite remarkable, always figuring him dressed up as peasant, presumably a sorcerer, and leading us into the incredible world of superstition of Le Berry. His work turns witchcraft into more of a tourist attraction than a social phenomenon, and actually merits study in itself. This type of literature characteristically focuses on the sorcerer and his/her spells. It also attributes credence in witchcraft indiscriminately to all local inhabitants, and deems witchcraft something one can speak of publicly to anyone curious enough to listen.[12] At best, such literature is entertaining,

---

12 Thus, reporter Rochet-Lucas tells how she met her first "witch" in 1981 during an "ethnological investigation." She bitterly regretted obtaining no proof of the encounter and of the many secrets revealed by the open-minded and hospitable witch, but unfortunately her tape recorder did not work that day (Rochet-Lucas 1991: 24-25).

Two postcards of Jean-Louis Boncoeur, "The Shepherd" and "La Parisienne"

though often just irritating. Nevertheless, it probably does find roots in local phenomena, although in this instance, the relationship between root and blossom is somewhat strange.

Mainly, it was what I encountered in the field spontaneously that led me to think discourses of witchcraft *did* exist in La Brumaire, though they were wisely wrapped in secrecy and privacy. As I said, I wasn't searching directly for witchcraft discourse, but I was certainly open to anything that might resemble it. I was dealing with what people said about others around them, and I often encountered ways of characterizing relations of power and reciprocal influence between neighbours that ran parallel to the way people in the Norman Bocage talked about spells. A word that frequently recurred in connection with this was "jealousy," as it had in Favret-Saada's descriptions. I have chosen to identify these non-magical discourses about neighbours as "parallel discourses," in reference to witchcraft.

Parallel discourses occurred sporadically in most daily talk, and reflected a general fear of others – their knowledge, influence and words – especially where relations were marked by jealousy and inequality, or by direct conflict. Along with what we have seen in the stories, conversation was full of expressions like, "watch out for them" (*...faut s'en mefier*); "They're just jealous..." (*C'est qu'ils sont jaloux...*); and, "Careful, they might get up to no good" (*Attention, ils peuvent devenir méchants*). Sometimes, indirect allusions to witchcraft like, "She knows things, she has books..." (*Elle sait des choses, elle a des livres...*) would occur, or – as when several small accidents befell members of the Association against reallotment – "Perhaps someone wants to do us harm" (*Il y a peut-être quelqu'un qui nous veut du mal*). Of course, such allusions were so indirect or encoded that the newcomer would never have suspected the talk to be about witchcraft, about discrediting someone through the symbolics of witchcraft.

Another similarity between Favret-Saada's descriptions and the talking in La Brumaire was the acting subject of the discourses. In the sorcery outlined by Favret-Saada, no one ever spoke of themselves as sorcerers. The discourse was only defensive, and only conducted by bewitched and unwitchers. Likewise, people in La Brumaire never talked about their own doings, only those of others. Only when talking about health problems would they engage in detailed personal descriptions. Again, as with sorcery, such talk was the defensive discourse of a victim.

We also saw examples in the stories, where the question of witchcraft is strongly evoked without actually being articulated. This is the case in the story about the Brigand sisters, where the second death and the time-lapse between them had a retroactive influence on the analysis of the first death, suddenly rendering it unnatural. Furthermore, the persons involved are relatives *and* neighbours, and as the situation has evolved, their already potentially difficult relations have become even more conflictual and subject to jealousy by the emergence of a new, third set of children. As a matter of fact, all subsequent cases of inheritance have been extremely painful, and even today, relations are very antagonistic. The various relatives are terribly tense about, and keep a close watch over, each other, and problems have naturally been articulated around the issue of the land reallotment, where family members find themselves in opposite camps – some for, some against, and some switching back and forth. During the last three years, there have been serious health problems in all three groups. At one point, it was said one old man had gone mad and his family was accusing his grand-nephew of rendering him so.[13] For a while, reactions were generally out of control, close to hysteria, everyone crying in public and violently accusing others of causing their own misfortune. Now it seems matters have calmed down because, finally, *everyone* feels cheated in the land reallotment, and therefore diverging factions have been able to find a kind of union and common ground, externalizing the conflict and identifying the Mayor and the administration as their common enemy.

The story of the Brigand sisters is obviously a witchcraft story, told as such to explain the very tense situation and clarify issues around the reallotment. If members of the family killed each other sixty years ago for land, they can be expected to react very violently today over the same matters. It is probable that current events have even shed new light on the old story and grounded suspicions of witchcraft – current

13 A piece of the old man's land had been attributed to the nephew by the land reallotment. The young man, who unlike his grand-uncle was against the land reallotment, eventually gave the piece of land back to him unofficially without getting anything in return. The nephew felt innocent since he had opposed the procedure, but knew if he kept the land, the old man would really go completely mad.

illnesses and mishaps being interpreted on the basis of the same old jealousy as further repetition and proof.

If the story of the Brigand sisters was only indirectly about sorcery, the story of Riolet's cows giving or not giving milk is explicit: "He had certain powers... He cast a spell" ("*Il avait des dons... Il l'a jeté un sort*"). Like in "The Brigand Sisters," it is probable this interpretation was only made after the same incident occurred twice. Cows do lose and regain their milk, but when the same person twice makes a dry cow give milk or a good milk cow dry out, it is no longer a coincidence. It is also typical of the tone of the story that the cows were "relational," changing owners and becoming part of another person's "vital force." Without this transfer (of force) there would have been no reason for accusing Riolet of "hocus-pocus."

More serious matters have also been explained, if not directly by witchcraft, by the jealousy of neighbours. At an early age, a young farmer inherited his father's farm and, just when many women were leaving the countryside to work in towns, he managed to marry a girl who was highly esteemed for her work capacity and discretion. All in all, he was a fortunate man. But the couple's first child died three days after birth without any evident symptoms of illness, the girl moved back to her parents and the farm started running into financial problems. After a while, the girl came back, things at the farm went better and they had another child. Today, the two hardly speak about it, but the infant's grave is always covered in flowers, and the farmer has directly (but without talking about spells) attributed the death of the child and the bad situation in general to the envy of his neighbours. Their continued decorating of the tomb twenty-five years later can be read as an ongoing manifestation of something like: "We might say hello to you on the road, but we still remember," and maybe even "You haven't heard the last of us."

In another clear-cut parallel discourse, a local artisan has several times evoked the tense relationship with certain neighbours he had as a very young man when he had to take over the family business because of his fathers sudden death:

> When I was hungry, they didn't want to help me... They did nasty things to me; they're mean... They tried to get me down, eh. They told my clients not

to buy from me, that I was Communist. But I held on, eh. And now they really see it didn't work, I'm still standing. Now they're jealous.[14]

This is similar to the discourses about spell-casting neighbours cited in Favret-Saada. First it is established that the neighbours are evil people, capable of wanting to injure others (they did not help a young man in distress); then that they actively tried to decrease his economic livelihood through the use of words; finally that their words were too weak, that he stood up to them and apparently even reversed the situation, outdoing them economically and increasing their jealousy. Furthermore, the fact that they are still jealous, that they are "bad," seems to be a warning, notifying the listener that they might try to strike again, since they never really got to him yet.

In Favret-Saada's descriptions, spells are directed toward health and livestock, always with the overall aim of diminishing the bewitched person's "capacity to produce, reproduce and survive" (Favret-Saada 1989: 43). This was obviously the case with the artisan also. The words "spell" and "sorcery" were not mentioned, but the means (words), the motivations (jealousy), the goal (economic ruin) and the mechanisms (by turning their force back on them, he outmanoeuvres them) are the same. The discourse here is more rational and less magical, but it still expresses the same fundamental themes: it is a relational discourse, involving inequality and jealousy, and demonstrating the influence and control fellow villagers can have on each other's lives.

Favret-Saada herself talks about a certain rationalization of witchcraft discourses in the Bocage as compared to the last century (1986: 45-46). Over time, certain religious elements and ideas about supernatural powers have disappeared from accounts, and other aspects, like their composition and rhetoric, have been modified. This is a result of what she calls "authentic cultural 'work' by the local society, the product of an incessant negotiation conducted with the dominant national culture"

---

14 *"Quand j'avais faim, ils ne voulaient pas m'aider." "Ils m'ont fait des méchancetés, c'est des mauvais." "Ils ont bien essayé de me faire tomber, hein. Ils disaient à mes clients qu'il fallait pas acheter chez moi, que j'étais communiste. Mais j'ai tenu, hein. Et maintenant, ils voient bien que ç'a pas marché, que je tiens debout. Maintenant ils sont jaloux."*

(ibid.: 29),[15] resulting in the invention of what she considers a new form of local psychotherapy (ibid.: 46). She identifies the therapeutic effect in the new ways of life that the status of being bewitched demands – where the bewitched person's position changes from inactive victim to hyperactive agent – and in the fact that what are often internal family problems are conceptualized and exteriorized by accusing neighbours (ibid.). Whereas in her original book (1977) she described and analyzed the internal logic of Bocage sorcery, in this later article (1986) she seems to want to explain how and why sorcery works from an external and somewhat rationalizing point of view.

Whether one can or should try to explain the mechanisms of witchcraft is doubtful. What is certain is that both the ancient and more recent discursive forms in the Bocage, as well as the discourses of La Brumaire, all reflect the same fundamental problems of neighbourhood: the control and power people have over their own and others' lives, lived out in a complex balance between dependence and independence.

The Power of Words
Essential and linked themes concerning communal life and relations are articulated by discourses of witchcraft in the Bocage and the Berry as well as by so-called parallel discourses: those of exchange and control, dependence and independence. These themes will be developed in the following chapter.

Furthermore, it is my opinion that Favret-Saada's "discourses of witchcraft" can actually be considered part of the larger phenomenon, "talking about neighbours," as we have seen above. In this sense, the recent rationalizations of discourse she describes should be conceived of as a reversible rather than irrevocable trend – a pendulum swing, allowing elements to disappear and recur with time. This would be quite similar to the historical transformations of Bakweri witchcraft described by Edwin Ardener (1970). He was able to establish that the articulation of beliefs in witches and zombies varied with economic conditions, where agricultural depression enhanced jealousy and provoked accusations of

---

15 "...un authentique 'travail' culturel de la société locale, le produit d'une incessante négotiation menée avec la culture nationale dominante."

zombie witchcraft. In the case of improved economic situations, such accusations would subside, and belief in witches would take another form. In his quite successful attempt to marry history and structure, he conceived of these variations as different expressions of the same fundamental structure or "template." Later, he referred to the template as a p-structure and to its actual expression as an s-structure: respectively, the paradigmatic and syntagmatic elements of, in this case, Bakweri witchcraft (1978: 90-93).

A possible parallel between witchcraft among the Bakweri and in France might be that one's fortune and misfortune is relative to other people's, and more generally, that according to other factors (e.g., political and economic), the theme of interdependence and control is articulated in more or less supernatural ways. In comparison with Ardener, I would not go so far as to call the fundamental theme developed in neighbour-discourses "structure": for the moment, "theme" or "relation" will do. With respect to Favret-Saada, the idea that rationalization might be reversible is only a guess. For the moment both Favret-Saada and I have only witnessed a tendency towards shedding magical elements and replacing them with more rational ones, not the reverse. Nevertheless, it is clear that the essential mechanisms of witchcraft are still present, and account for events in people's lives. Furthermore, it is possible that similar rationalizing and de-rationalizing has taken place in other historical periods of which we have little or no knowledge. The rationalization process described by Favret-Saada is influenced by an official discourse that condemns supernatural explanations of health and well-being, and one might very well imagine that similar discourse-"correction" could have taken place during strong periods of inquisition, when the lives of individuals and communities were at stake.[16] Finally, as we see in Favret-Saada's work, sorcery in the Bocage is not an isolated rural phenomenon. The unwitchers solicited are in some cases city folks who read the future in crystal balls and tarotcards. It would therefore be wrong to isolate such sorcery from the whole movement of spiritual therapy that has been flourishing lately

---

16 Evidence of such changes in discourse could probably be found in literature from the Inquisition periods, but it would require very careful investigation since such literature, called "the archives of oppression" (*les archives de la repression*) by Muchembled (1991: 40), always reflects the official view. Such a task is beyond my scope here.

under diverse guises – a movement that has had its up and downs, but apparently never completely disappears.

I am not sure to what extent Ardener makes a distinction between, on one hand, using magical symbolics and holding neighbours responsible for hardships endured, and on the other, using more rational symbolics but still holding neighbours responsible. Maybe the Bakweri just stop accusing each other of their misfortune altogether because they are better off in general. Maybe the "amount" of witchcraft just generally diminishes. What is certain, however, is that while the symbolics of witchcraft may vary, a certain repetitive, structuring tendency – that of "relating persons to misfortune through other persons" – remains constant (1989: 89-91).

In La Brumaire, the power of words seems to remain equally strong whether magic is involved or not. Witchcraft symbolics are not often employed. Nevertheless, people seem to be just as careful about what they say about their neighbours, where and to whom they say it, as they are when they do use witchcraft symbolics, and as people are in the situations described by Favret-Saada. Obviously, words are still just as potent, even in "rational" speech.

According to Favret-Saada, Malinowski identified a particular type of discourse, "*communion phatique*," that was meant not to inform but to establish and maintain communication between interlocutors by encompassing weather, health and other anodyne subjects (1977: 27, n. 9). But I was never able to identify such distinctly non-important talk during my stay in La Brumaire. People do talk about weather and health, but never in a careless way, and the simple act of talking together is charged with meaning. Subjects can be more or less hot, but talk itself is never cold. As with silence, *potential* information is always an inherent part of "cool" chatting. Favret-Saada compares such talk in the Bocage to a temporary ceasefire: "It conveys to one's interlocutor that one *might* launch a magic rocket at him, but that one chooses not to do so for the time being" (1980: 10; italics mine).[17] What is not being said is constantly evoked by what *is* said.

We still haven't come much closer to an explanation of *why* and *how*

---

17 "...c'est faire savoir à son interlocutor qu'on pourrait lui balancer une fusée magique, mais qu'on préfère la retenir provisoirement" (1977: 27).

words are powerful, to an understanding of the mechanisms. Nor does establishing that words are powerful explain silence. Words and silence are both equally strong elements of discourse, as we shall see further on. What is sure is that, as isolated symbols, words have no power. They must always be connected to specific persons, and thus to a social relation between the speaker and the person talked about, in order to work. Words may exist for centuries as inert signs on the pages of sacred books, but only when someone falls upon them, when they are spoken out loud and directed towards someone – only when they are inscribed in a network of social relations – do they become alive and potent.

In witchcraft, powerful words are applied to pre-existing and unbalanced relations. Such words comment on the social; but they are also capable of working (and intended to work) on this social situation to change it. In the same way, words in La Brumaire are never spoken just to inform, they are also spoken with an intent to change things.

This sets them against the words used in rumours, which were tentatively defined above (Chapter 2) as stories about people *outside* both the narrator's and the listeners' field of tension, and thus influence. The knowledge obtained through rumour and the words that convey it are not vectors of power or mutual influence. The "gossip columns" of tabloid magazines might make their readers feel that they harbour valuable knowledge and stand at a privileged, "gossipy distance" from the rich and famous whose exploits and mishaps are revealed. But such knowledge is without social significance – it is blunt, impotent. It has nothing to do with a social relationship, nor with the explosive potency of exchanging words about one's neighbours, friends, relatives and enemies in La Brumaire.

To understand the relationship between dependence and independence and the phenomenon of mutual control, a closer look at the phenomenon of exchange itself might be more fruitful than focusing on the commodity exchanged: words. In the next chapter, the general principles and conditions of the exchange of things, deeds and words will be developed; and specific cases where conditions allowed me to be admitted as an interlocutor in discourses of neighbourship (and therein of witchcraft) will be exposed. Then, after examining both words as social signifiers and their modes of change, the next step will be to look at the content of words – the knowledge actually conveyed – because the concrete, social situation of exchange, where people perform knowledge and define themselves and others as interlocutors, is one thing; the knowledge itself is another. If words are powerful, it is largely due to the power of the knowledge they hold and convey.

3.3 Exchanging: Goods, Deeds, Words

As I noted in my introduction, a high level of self-sufficiency prevails in La Brumaire, and is linked to a system of internal exchange. The official monetary system now dominates many transactions, mainly those connected to the outside world (like cattle- and grain-trading and the payment of pensions), but a great deal of internal circulation of goods, deeds, help, etc. still takes place. Some local artisans even prefer being paid at least partly in kind, if not completely. And when it comes to giving gifts, home-made products characteristically serve as gifts to others rather than items obtained commercially. Typical gifts are fruits, vegetables, eggs, and sometimes home-made alcohol – and blood sausage:

At the annual pig-slaughtering, it is customary to give pieces of blood sausage (black pudding) to family, close friends and neighbours. Everyone follows the same local recipe, the only variation being in the amount of onions used, which makes the sausage more or less soft (*moelleux*). Pieces are quite small, one might even say symbolic, but giving them is very important, especially to the right persons. In the end, when everyone has made and distributed their blood sausage, the count comes out even, everyone receiving just as much as they gave. It can be added that blood-sausage-giving follows the rules of delayed exchange in that special attention is given to supplying sausage – albeit a very small amount – to households that have not yet finished their slaughtering, or did so some time earlier.

From an economic point of view, this sausage circulation is quite useless and does not even help disseminate new recipes since the sausages are all the same; but from a social point of view, the exchange clearly follows the lines of Maussian gift-giving since it is guided by formal reciprocity and, to some extent, even contractual obligation (Mauss 1954: 1-5). It is obvious that this dealing in bits of sausage is a very rudimentary form of the extensive exchange in things and women that Mauss, and later Lévi-Strauss, described as being at the basis of social life and human society. But just as Mauss traces elements of the principles of archaic exchange in modern society (ibid.: passim) in a way that could be inscribed within Ardener's distinction between "program" (p-structure) and "output" (s-structure) (1989:55) – and thus likened to the way talking about neighbours takes on different, sometimes magical, forms – blood-sausage-giving is obviously more than just a reminiscence of traditional ways or a following of norms. Giving sausage is still – today maybe more than ever – a deliberate and active way of establishing (temporary) relations: of confirming or weakening pre-existing alliances and creating new ones. Within their specific social field of tension, every household delineates their personal alliance- and solidarity-group. What's more, they delineate it *in blood*.[18] If asked why they were giving away all their blood sausage, people in La Brumaire would probably answer: "Because that's what's done" (*Parce que ça se fait*). Meanwhile, they are very well aware of the symbolic implications of their gesture.

On a smaller scale and of a more immediate nature, wine exchange has some of the same implications: wine (preferably red) is incessantly shifted around, mainly at bistro tables, where everyone buys a round and receives a glass from each of the others'. No one leaves until all the rounds have been finished, and no one can refuse an offered glass – no one except a woman that is, since wine exchange takes place mainly between men. Social drinking rounds are daily fare where men go to bistros, but their importance as a sign of alliance is accentuated in La Brumaire. Unlike blood-sausage-giving, social drinking takes place any time of year, and thus keeps people abreast of current affairs. Also, like giving blood sausage, sharing wine carries the symbolics of sharing blood.[19]

18 This exchange could also be compared to ritual-like blood exchanges, where mixing blood changes a bond of friendship into a consanguin relation ("the same blood now runs in our veins").
19 During the reallotment conflict, the fact that almost everyone in the village was an active member in the blood donors' association became a problem. They were all giving blood into the same huge pool. Unlike other cross-divided groupings where co-operation seemed to be less problematic despite the conflict, blood-doning villagers often chose not to continue giving blood or participate in the blood-donor banquets.

Exchanges like wine-sharing and blood-sausage-giving are perhaps all the more important today, since many other ways of manifesting alliances have diminished as currency-based transactions increase and farm machinery reduces the size of work-teams. But many goods and deeds are still exchanged in La Brumaire without the intermediary of money, and many specialized services can still be paid partly or totally in kind. Of course, this is the case in most places, even big cities, where a kind of parallel economy coexists with the official, legal one. But in La Brumaire, these economies are not really distinct and parallel, they are integrated, and together they constitute the internal or local economy.

The exchange of deeds or labour is very widespread and, in terms of economics, probably has larger implications than the exchange of goods. This holds true for both farmers and non-farmers. Help is given to shift herds from one field to another, and calling the veterinarian is avoided as neighbours help with difficult calvings, medical treatments and vaccinations, some farmers being quite adept at handling injection needles. Many farming households count only one, or at the most two, active persons, which is nowhere near enough for large tasks like planting, sowing, harvesting, silage and sheep-shearing. During these periods, everyone depends heavily on others' help, and if they cannot count on it they risk losing their harvest.

At such times, the importance of having allies and being on good terms with one's neighbours becomes most obvious, and allegiance plays itself out most clearly as a means of defining relations between oneself and others. Because most of these activities take place out in the open (unlike gift-giving for example), they are public statements. Thus, working alliances are not only contractual expressions between two parties, they are open expositions of current allegiances, written directly in the landscape by groups of bodies working together in the fields.

Along the same lines, omitting to help someone who expects or solicits help is dangerous. It is an obvious breach in relations and hence demands careful consideration because it is so conspicuous, and because everyone depends on mutual help. Clearly, Durand did not help Carreteau bring in the hay this year, although Carreteau helped Durand with his harvest. Durand must have his reasons, Carreteau must have done or said something wrong. If not, Durand is sliding, being negligent. To be further investigated!

Exchanging deeds.

Taking a break in the fields.

From an analytical point of view, helping fellow villagers might seem more naturally necessary and less symbolically interesting than the almost ritual distribution of blood sausage, but upon closer investigation, simple day-to-day transactions and cooperation manifest the same fundamental ideas about reciprocal exchange and interdependence. As one villager very simply expressed it: "If you want a helping hand, you must lend one."[20] And when furthermore he says: "People who get along help each other out,"[21] he demonstrates both the relationship between a virtual or abstract social relation and its actual expression, and on another level, the way that such expressions are constantly being analyzed. There exist here both a simple notion of causality that is, furthermore, reversible (cooperation implying good relations and vice versa), and an awareness of such causal logic being applied.

Local Principles of Exchange

All exchanges in La Brumaire, whether in words, deeds or goods, seem to delineate and follow the same principles. Principles *per se* can be neither seen nor heard but are nevertheless always present. In looking for them, one detects only their concrete expression (c.f. Ardener 1978: 90). In some situations, these principles stand out more clearly or make themselves more obvious than in others, on the level of both participation and analysis. They become what Ardener characterized as "significant events" (1978). As we have seen, Brumairian principles of exchange seem to be crystallized in blood-sausage exchange and wine sharing for example, and are also very common in stories where they are articulated around some specific themes:

Enough vs. Too Much

As we have seen above, one persistent local theme is the balance between having "enough" and having "too much." In the story of Fields (13), we saw how Thérèse had to burn her hay in order not to have too much, and later on, how Mme. Colin was ashamed, almost frightened,

20 "*Quand on veut des coups de main, il faut en donner.*"
21 "*Ceux qui sont bien ensemble, ils se donnent des coups de main.*"

of having had too good a harvest from someone else's land.

"Having" is closely connected to "giving" and exchange, both in Mauss's various descriptions (1954) and in La Brumaire. When giving, one shows, performs one's potential, what one has. In a system of reciprocity, giving implies having, and to have, to get, one must give. But in La Brumaire, just as one should only have just enough, one should never give too much either. An effort is always made to give just the right amount, neither too much nor too little. This runs counter to the principle of excessive gift-giving of potlatch and to some extent Kula exchange as described by Mauss (ibid.) and that of the Moka described by Ongka (1979) for example, where one of the aims is to bestow gifts of an amount and value far exceeding the recipient's capacity to repay. In Mauss's analysis, potlatch gift-giving is meant to demonstrate superiority and subordination and establish hierarchy (1954: 72).

By contrast, great attention is paid in La Brumaire to preserving the recipient's honour, and gift-giving is not really intended to outdo the receiver, although to some extent it does contain an element of challenge. But giving something one thinks the recipient is unable to repay is considered extremely arrogant.

In witchcraft and its parallel discourses, we have seen how a person's health and wealth is relative to that of others, and how they are constantly being transferred. Thus, having something means depriving someone else of having it. This idea is stated in the phrase, "His good fortune was based on the misfortune of someone else,"[22] referring to the adopted orphan who inherited farm and land after the death of his adoptive parents' biological son, and indicating a balance between the good fortune of one and the misfortune of another. Overall, it seems as though there were only a certain amount of health and wealth to go around, and that taking too big a part from the common pool would violate a ruling principle of equality.

In this way, and in line with Favret-Saada's ideas about the transfer of vital force (1977), the case of a young couple who lost their first child just as their farm was starting to yield a surplus can be interpreted as a re-equilibration of an unbalanced situation. In terms of causality, the

---

22 *"Il a fait son bonheur sur le malheur d'un autre."*

moral of the event would be that the excessive vitality of the overly happy household was dispelled (by envious neighbours) to re-establish a balance. But although the Bocage logic in Favret-Saada's descriptions certainly looks like this kind of ethno-functionalism, the equilibrium model does not render a satisfactory account of the general principle of Brumairian reciprocity. Although the idea of causality most probably exists in the analysis of such events as the death of a child, it does not mean that exchange is carried out to maintain balance. In fact, Brumairians are not particularly democratic or egalitarian, and are not always trying to share wealth equally among themselves. As we have seen, considerable differences in the wealth of individuals and households persist.

Nevertheless, whereas Kwakiutl and Trobrianders give gifts to dismiss and place themselves *above* others, Brumairians give gifts to maintain a balance of some order. In both instances, although in opposite ways, gift-giving deals with and expresses a reciprocal relation between people. Where the functionalist idea of an overall balance deals with wholes, reciprocity in La Brumaire deals with relations between individuals and families.

Although I speak of principles as if they existed overtly in Brumairian culture, obviously they are not apparent to the newcomer beyond their actual enactment. Principles of exchange become evident to the ethnographer through concrete cases of exchange, and are actually most clear when *not* pursued. Events that would otherwise be considered obvious or banal and perhaps be overlooked by the newcomer suddenly stand out as exceptional, like a "cultural text written in neon." Thus, when one woman gave a hand-polished crystal wine glass to compensate for breaking quite a simple glass at a neighbour's house, she went terribly overboard, and ultimately put the relationship at risk. The recipient was put in a position where she could not possibly reciprocate, and furthermore, the gift very effectively put the two in their respective places – one an educated city woman, the other a peasant girl – almost as well as words could have done, one unable to answer the other in her language. The much too precious compensation was quickly hidden, left unanswered because it was unanswerable.

As for possession, and wealth in general, Brumairians take great care not to reveal what they have as far as income, land and savings are concerned, again as if "having" were suspicious. One might even say that having belongs to a supposedly private domain of existence. Unlike the Corsicans in Knudsen's descriptions (1989a), flaunting wealth is clearly avoided in La Brumaire. Better to drive an old, carefully preserved and mended car than a shiny new one for all to see. The effort invested in repairing an old car is preferable to the effort spent earning the money to buy a new (or newer) one. That these cars might one day be worth a fortune, some of them dating from the fifties and in very good shape, does not enter into consideration apparently. In general, buying new agricultural machines is also problematic, for on one hand they are tools for work so the investment is justified and younger farmers are willing to go into debt to acquire them; but on the other hand, farm machines are still considered a performance of wealth. That the money to buy them is borrowed from the bank partly saves face, but it is also a problem, since being unable to pay from one's own pocket shows *lack* of potential and independence.

Likewise, a person's land potential is protected from outside inquiry and talked about in vague terms. Owning land is important and cherished, but even in connection with the reallotment it was impossible to find out exactly how much land people had at their disposal since rented and borrowed land, which often constituted a larger area than the land they owned outright, did not figure in the official lists. It is symptomatic that when I once helped a farmer fill out some draught-compensation forms and hence came to know exactly how much land he disposed of, my position in the family changed radically. I had been made privy to very private knowledge. Secrecy as to one's potential – land, savings, wages – might derive in part from a respect for the principle of balance, since overly precise figures would clearly show if such balance were being neglected.

Closely linked to the ideas of enough and too much is the game of making another overstep the line in what I choose to call "tug-of-war" games.

Tug-of-War
In the well known game, tug-of-war, opponents face each other, both pulling hard on opposite ends of a rope until the weaker party loses con-

trol and is pulled over the forbidden dividing line. While the point of the game is to show muscle, in La Brumaire skill and self-control are revealed, and eventually the opponent's lack of these – not through rope-pulling, but by exchanging words and alcohol. In one case, the object is to make the opponent give too much, in the other, to take (in) too much:

Although drinking and exchanging drinks is, as we have seen, a convenient way to show who one's allies are in public, it is also a means of confronting and challenging them. What social drinkers must prove is that they control the situation: not that they can drink without limit and remain upright, but that they can prevent others from making them drink too much. One cannot refuse a glass, every glass must be emptied and any verbal attempt to control its content is completely overheard. But one can prevent it being filled to the rim by lifting it as it is filled. The person pouring will lift the bottle too, resulting in a vertical tug-of-war, bottle and glass rising to the sky. Eventually the flow stops, but what determines the amount in the glass is not so much arm-length or the law of gravity, as speed, determination and control. What is at stake is not how much or how little alcohol a person can take, but how he (or, rarely, she) protects his own limits, in this case, limits of alcohol consumption. It goes without saying that newcomers like myself come to learn this by experience.[23]

"Tugs-of-wine" are quite simple to spot since they are so visibly staged in time and space: companions seated around a table with a bottle and some wine glasses. The curtain rises on the event at around the time they sit down, and falls again when they get up to leave. "Tugs-of-word" follow the same rules, but they are much more difficult to detect since words can be exchanged anywhere at any time. In fact, the element of tugging is always present as an underlying principle in any conversation but it develops into an actual game only rarely. Nevertheless, framing the dynamic in these terms makes it clearer, and moreover, when I detected tugging, it was often because I myself was being tested, and in such cases, things did somehow take on the dimension of a game – like when cats play with mice: a game, but a serious one.

---

[23] Women, especially newcomers, will sometimes be offered a drink, but after much insistence and resistance, "No, thank you" is usually acceptable. This does not hold true for men, nor for women who already accepted once.

The general idea of the word-tug is to make the other give too much information, lose control and "spill the beans." Since we are talking about exchange, "too much" is relative to what one gives oneself. We have seen how much energy is put into discretion and withholding words, and in what terms affluent talking is described. Whereas terms like *"causant"* (chatty), *"bavard"* (talkative) and *"pipelette"* (natterer) are generally used in the case of unwelcome talk, tug-of-word implies a deliberate provocation of talkativeness. It also implies that one does oneself talk. As in tug-of-wine, there is a real challenge. The winner is the one who has given the least and received the most information, and has thus made the other interlocutor "spill."

As for most talking, there also exist expressions (always a big help to the ethnographic detective in her work) about verbal tug-of-war, though they are not articulated in terms of war. For example, "He wanted to get it out of me"[24] clearly means that "he," the other, wanted the speaker to say more than was due, wanted to take the words right out of his mouth without "paying" for them. "She's good at finding things out, that one"[25] implies that knowing requires exchange skills, releasing little to obtain a lot.

Tug-of-word is exercised in much the same way as fishing, both following and underlining ideas about patience and silence, as well as sharing the aspect of pleasure experienced when a big "fish" bites. A little piece of bait – a worm or a ball of bread – is put on the hook, and the fisherman waits until a small fish bites. Then the little fish is used as bait to catch a bigger fish, and so on. In the same way, the "word-angler" lets drop a little information, just enough to get the other going, and then skilfully keeps the conversation alive without actually saying much him/herself. And when someone has passed a test intended to make them over-talk, they are said to have not bitten the bait, *"Il n'a pas mordu."* It actually seems that tug-of-word could be distinguished from other forms of word exchange when clearly defined roles of "fish" and "fisherman" are being played. Unlike the principle of reciprocity, and like pulling fish out of the sea, the flow of information in word-angling is ideally one-way. But opposing the principle does not

24 *Il voulait m'arracher quelques mots.*
25 *Elle est forte pour savoir, celle-là.*

invalidate it, on the contrary: tugs-of-war overtly play on and express the principle of reciprocity, without which there would be no challenge, only lifeless flow – or lack of communication altogether. Thus with both wine and words, the quest for reciprocity can be inverted or stretched to its extreme, and the enough/too much principle reoriented.

Some final remarks about principles of exchange: it is now clear that exchange implies reciprocity. But reciprocity does not necessarily mean that one should repay in the same currency that one received, as in the classical examples of Maussian gift-giving where pigs are traded for pigs and bracelets for necklaces. On the contrary, deeds can make up very well for goods, goods for words, and so on. Reciprocity implies equivalence in value, not necessarily in kind. This became especially clear in my access to knowledge, as we shall see.

Furthermore, exchange also has to do with withholding, and just as there is meaningful silence, there is also meaningful refusal to exchange. Refusal is by definition a reaction to an expectation or a challenge. But whereas refusal to receive in Mauss's analysis (1954: 40) and Knudsen's description of Corsican silence (1989b: 51) implies that the defied person (or potential receiver) feels superior to the defier (giver) and rejects the challenge (the gift), in La Brumaire such refusal usually means that the relation is altered or cut. This does not mean there is no longer a relation – the two persons still belong within each other's field of tension and are still potential allies or enemies – but that it has been negatively charged.

A short comment on selling beef: only twenty years ago, the market was a place for meeting and competing, not only to determine who had the best animals, but also who sold them at the highest prices. In the marketplace, men and women publicly negotiated animals, but in doing so also put themselves at stake, negotiating their relative positions and making allies. Today, cattle prices are set by the E.E.C. They are no longer negotiated, relative and subjective values, and this is strongly regretted. Lack of a marketplace means lack of negotiation and competition, and probably lack of opportunity to make allies further away than those living in the immediate surroundings.

In order to grasp some of the fundamentals of word exchange, it has been useful to look at principles of exchange in general, especially because words can be exchanged for goods and deeds, and vice versa. By examining specific transactions and talking about exchange, I have tried to nail down some principles.

To really see a principle in action, to follow the exchange of a thing, it would be convenient to be able mark it with a radioactive isotope like biochemists do to see the metabolism of a specific molecule in an organism. But how do you mark knowledge or words? I once tried to follow the dissemination of a story from the moment I knew it came into existence. The postman entered my mother-in-law's house almost unannounced. We did not see him arrive, and had not had time to put things in order. Our orphan donkey foal had been put up for the night next to the living room fireplace, and during the night had pissed on a heap of newspapers laid down for that purpose just inside the front door. To enter the room, the postman had to step over the wet newspapers and the donkey foal, which he did with no apparent consternation or comment. He just sat down as usual and had his cup of coffee. But it is absolutely certain that as soon as he got to the next house, the event became a great story. But whereas biochemists have isotopes that readily reveal themselves, I should have known that I, as one of the persons up for discussion, would never hear of the incident again, although everyone around me now knew about it.

My Access to Knowledge

These reflections on exchange are based mainly on three different and intertwined types of information: 1) what I could observe going on in the village, like blood-sausage-giving; 2) what people said about exchange, giving, receiving and helping; 3) direct experience from exchanges in which I took part.

Over the last couple of decades, anthropology has come to acknowledge that the data anthropologists sample during fieldwork, and with which they subsequently work, are not neutral facts but subjectively lived experience (e.g., Clifford & Marcus 1986; Hastrup 1992; Turner 1986). This is also true of the material presented and analyzed here. Hence, the following passage, which outlines specific situations in which I became a partner in exchange, either in goods, deeds or words, is not meant to contribute yet another illustration of the subjective and personal nature of the fieldwork. It is intended to further an understanding of the ways in which the position of a person is stated, commented upon and readjusted in actual exchange, taking advantage of the fact that I have front-row insight into one of the exchange partners – myself – at least as regards what I did and said to become who and what I am.

Who and what I am is never something fixed though, and it is certainly not because I am me that "I know best" – perhaps the contrary. The interpretation of what I did and said is only revealed in bits and pieces and through subtle indicators, especially to me. But in that respect, I am no different from others in La Brumaire. That is one reason why there is only subjectively lived experience and no overall neutral facts; no person could ever reasonably describe what a person actually *is*, but at most, how that being *becomes*. This is not only an epistemological condition but an overall theoretical stance. Nothing simply is, it is constantly becoming.

As we have already seen in the introduction, when I started my inquiry into the lives of Brumairians, I was a newcomer but not a stranger. A stranger is someone who has not yet given or been assigned a common impression, cannot be neatly placed on a shelf or conceived of in local terms and definitions as anything other than an outsider. I could be because I was the daughter-in-law of an inhabitant (albeit an uncommon one), and because I took a clear stance in the land conflict. Moreover, I was non-French and a woman, which entailed certain other expectations of my behaviour on the part of the local people. But how I actually moved, and was moved, around on my roughly designated shelf remained to be seen and investigated as occasions arose.

The land reallotment procedure very conveniently separated out part of the population of La Brumaire and set me in special relation to it. Almost everyone whose concerns lay within the perimeter of expropriated land had a standpoint for or against and consequently became either opposed or allied to me by definition. This was not intentional, it followed as a natural part of being involved. Because, like everyone involved in the conflict, and like all Corsicans involved in a vendetta (Knudsen 1989a: 186), I was expected to choose sides. Conversely, if I had not chosen sides, I would not have existed socially, and I would have had absolutely no access to knowledge.

People mixed up my filmmaking work, my fieldwork and the reallotment issues, which was actually quite reasonable since they were indeed interlaced: without the film, we (my husband and I) would not have been involved in the conflict, without the conflict we would not have made the film, and without both, I would not have carried out the fieldwork that I did. As events progressed, we assumed the role of village scribes, the "schooled" ones people turn to when they have to communicate in a language or a discursive mode that is not their own, and who keep track of events in the village. In that sense we were performing an important local function, whereas the fieldwork alone would not have been a reason for being there and finding things out. As Favret-Saada writes, one cannot ask without reason, just for the sake of knowing.

In my integrated function as filmmaker/scribe/fieldworker, I went visiting, and in almost every case, when I left I was given a gift: a sack of potatoes, a pumpkin, lettuce, eggs, cream, a bottle of "home-brew," or something of the sort. I was obviously conceived of as performing a function that the gifts were meant to repay, to avoid indebtedness. Thus deeds were repaid with or exchanged for goods. Furthermore, on another level, the size and type of the gift, or the lack of one, also said something about the nature of my visit – how it was received – and about the concurrent state of reciprocity. Sometimes people seemed to judge that their participation in the film or their information in itself was enough: their words repaid my deeds. At other times, they believed they had received unpaid help, and that my effort demanded a recompense. Either way, the contribution of every participant was carefully measured. For skilled information-dealers like Brumairians, words and information acquire very accurately estimated values. I did not need ethical scruples, I was getting nothing for free. Although apparently people did not care much about my ethnographic inquiry, they knew that it dealt with neighbours, talking and knowledge, and that I depended on their support to succeed.

Apart from these direct exchanges, people would also come to our house with presents. They knew that organizing and evaluating opposition to the land reallotment was generating lots of paperwork for us ("You're not being paid; a lawyer would be..."), and they tried to compensate for this according to their means with gifts and help in the garden. For a certain period of time, they felt they had not contributed enough, that the balance was uneven, perhaps because we were working within a discursive domain that was not theirs – which is why they came to my mother-in-law in the first place – and for which they had no equivalent "currency," and because they could hardly pay us like they would have an unknown lawyer.

That the land reallotment defined me as a possible, sometimes even necessary, exchange-partner became quite evident simply because it did not define me as such for everyone. People who were not touched by or involved in the conflict felt no necessity to exchange either goods, deeds nor words with me, and our relations were not "charged" or under tension. Having an indirect connection with people who had become acquaintances of my mother-in-law over time was not enough to establish a direct or defined relationship with them. The secondary implication of this was that I heard fewer stories about them – not that I heard none at all, but since these people were not involved in the conflict, it was deemed that I need not know about them. In this respect, even though they might be close neighbours, they were "too far away" to be of concern.

The field of tension established around me this way by the land reallotment, within which there could be talking and silence, giving and withholding – in short, exchange – recalls Favret-Saada's concept of being *"pris,"* taken in or caught. For like her, without being *"prise,"* involved, I was subject to no exchange and had no access to knowledge. I am not claiming that my specific field of tension was as charged as Favret-Saada's was. She was dealing with "high voltage" – death, accidents and grave illness. Sometimes she was *"supposée pouvoir,"* supposed to be able to deflect powers back to their sources, sometimes *"supposée victime,"* a supposed victim, affected by them in turn. The observation I want to make by comparing our experiences is that whenever ethnographers and anthropologists deal with social relations, in some way they must also participate in them. Staying "outside" to preserve their overview limits their experience and hence the kind of information gathered. Slightly modifying Favret-Saada's concepts around this situation, I therefore think I could have been considered *prise* in the conflict over land, both as a victim and, more importantly, as an unwitcher – or in this case, an "unreallotter."

This idea was confirmed when we met Monsieur Febvre. Febvre was a farmer in a neighbouring village who was also fighting a local reallotment. He had been a member of the Commission, but had withdrawn after overhearing a discussion between two other Commission members planning how to get their hands on the best pieces of land. In the mind of Mr. Febvre, the reallotment was a conspiracy, the work of jealous neighbours who wanted to hurt him. He told us how, as a young man, he had fallen ill, poisoned, and how afterwards he switched to non-chemical agriculture. He has his cows treated by a medium, *un intermédiaire*, who uses plants, various other objects, and formulas. Febvre uses holy water from Lourdes to protect himself and his animals, and himself cured a man of a wart, although he claims to have no powers. He believes in sorcery: his family has been victim to all kinds of evils and spells cast by jealous neighbours. His uncle lost everything because of sorcery: first his harvests failed, then his animals died, and in the end he had to sell the farm. They found a photo of him: "I don't know how this was taken. He had a needle here, close to his heart."[26] "I believe in sorcery."[27]

I was of course puzzled by Mr. Febvre's spontaneous outpouring about sorcery, on one hand so close to Favret-Saada's descriptions, and on the other, so distant. We had come neither as annunciators nor unwitchers, and he had no reason to talk to us about his worries. He was probably just delirious. But on second thought, from his point of view the reallotment was the result of sorcery, he saw the two as one. In that sense, we who had come to talk with him about fighting the reallotment, that is, fighting neighbours, were indeed unwitchers. We also looked like people he already knew, Mme. Flora and *"Le mage de la Sousterraine"* (the wizard of Sousterraine). We had special knowledge and mastered a domain of discourse that was not his. As Favret-Saada wrote: "It was my interlocutors who decided what my position was (*'caught'* or not, bewitched or unwitcher) by interpreting unguarded clues in my speech" (1980: 17).[28] Febvre saw us come to him like that, ourselves victims and adversaries of jealous neighbours as well as ap-

---

26 "*Je ne sais pas comment ça a été pris, il avait une aiguille ici, près du coeur.*"
27 "*La sorcellerie, moi, je crois à ça.*"
28 "*Ce furent mes interlocuteurs qui me désignèrent ma place («prise» ou non, ensorcelée ou désenvoûteuse) en interprétant les signes involontaires que leur offrait mon discours*" (1977: 38).

parent masters of the discourse of power, and he judged it necessary for us to know all.

Another incident reinforced the idea that being *prise* could sometimes apply to us: our donkey got a wart. The veterinarian sometimes came to our house to check my mother-in-law's donkeys. Once I dropped by his drugstore, we started discussing local ways, and I told him about my research. When he came to have a look at Penelope's wart a couple of days later, he said: "I can treat the symptoms and take the wart away, but it will come back. To make it go away for good, you should see a healer." He had never mentioned alternative treatments before, but because I told him a few days earlier that I believed there were several valid ways of treating illness, he could now talk openly about it without looking silly.

I also talked to a shopkeeper about the warts, and she knew the veterinarian was coming. So when she asked how it all went, I told her what he had said. This immediately led to her recounting that her own horse had recently developed a wart near its eye which had been cured by a healer, a *guérisseuse*, who just moved her hands around in the air, pronouncing some formulas. The shopkeeper had talked about the horse's wart several times, about how a veterinarian had operated on it and how it kept coming back, but she had never told me about the *guérisseuse* before. Only after the account of Penelope's wart had been inscribed within a discourse on the supernatural could the woman talk to me in kind, as someone *prise*.

Other people reacted the same way when they heard how I had assimilated the idea of curing. They eventually revised versions of events they had already told me about, and admitted that they knew people who consulted *guérisseurs* and others who believed in sorcery. I was eventually told about people in the area and even in the village who could cure shingles ("*zonas*"), burns, insect- and snake-bites, as well as about an old woman, now deceased, who had cured a neighbour when he woke up one morning with his fist inextricably clenched, and hence unable to work. The doctor could not help him and after a month or so he finally went to see the *guérisseuse* who opened his hand.

I came to hear of an old woman who could see a sorcerer's face on the surface of the water in her bucket, and toward the end of my stay, it was even admitted that the woman was in fact my interlocutor's grandmother. I was told the story of the baker in a neighbouring town whose bread had recently stopped rising. He eventually sought the aid of a *guérisseur*, a priest it was said, who told him to put a black cock in his barn to repel the evil. This did not help, though: the sorcerer was stronger, and one day the baker was found dead, hanging from a rope in his barn, the cock strutting about beneath him. His tragic death was mentioned in the local press. Before, people only told me what I could read in the newspaper, as though it were their only source as well. Now they added the information about the bread that would not rise, the curing priest and the black cock, which indeed made it look less like a simple case of suicide.

Nevertheless, even though people would admit having heard about sorcery, it was almost always in another village, and they would never admit having themselves been implicated. Why should they, to someone like me who was obviously neither an ignorant victim who needed advice, nor a fighter of magical powers? Only as an "unreallotter" was I addressed and invited to help.

Several features differentiated common attitudes toward healing from those regarding sorcery. Although people did not talk about their own experiences with sorcery, they did eventually talk about going to see *guérisseurs* or healers. Even though these healers used magic formulas and had special *"dons"* (i.e., were gifted), the mechanisms of causality and repetition and the social dimension of witchcraft – jealousy and influence, and attributing responsibility to neighbours – seemed to be lacking. Using healers was still not openly talked about either, but could be mentioned as an alternative to official medicine, even by doctors and veterinarians, when someone was suffering from something.

I hardly think, though, that a clear-cut distinction between healing and sorcery can really be established. Both belong to a whole complex of Christian and probably pre-Christian ideas about good, evil, and the divine and diabolical powers that can be evoked by humans. In either case, the misery comes from outside. In healing, the transfer of power remains vertical, an issue arising between the divine and the victim, and the healer, the sacred advocate (the *intermédiaire*), implores the divinity to get things back to normal. In sorcery, humans have seized the powers, have made them theirs, and the power transfer becomes horizontal, between sorcerers, bewitched and unwitchers. It is no surprise that the

Catholic church rejects this horizontalization, the civilian seizure of divine powers without intermediaries, and that priests who take on unwitching in addition to spiritual protecting are reprimanded, although also accepted to a certain degree because they are still functioning within the system as members of the clergy. The borderline between unwitching and just healing is indistinct, and to know about either, one had to be *pris*.

In light of Favret-Saada's work and my own experiences, I can talk about being *prise* in two steps, for it seems to me that there are two different obstacles to talking about curing and witchcraft. At first, people are afraid of looking silly and backward, but once the newcomer herself acknowledges the irrationality of illness, the limits of "modern" medicine and the value of healing, the first obstacle is overcome. Secondly, although people will admit to having heard about sorcery and unwitchers and knowing others who have sought the aid of a healer for minor problems, they will most probably never speak of their own problems within the logic of witchcraft unless they are talking to someone who is presumably either powerful ("able") or afflicted (a victim).

Favret-Saada does not really distinguish between these two obstacles, but her own work centres on situations where both were overcome. I did not experience big difficulties overcoming the first obstacle because I openly expressed my belief that many if not all illnesses are psychologically and (mainly) socially conditioned, that the will to defy an illness is the main requisite for curing it, and that cures that take social and psychological conditions into consideration are the most effective. The relentlessly clenched fist of the man mentioned above was obviously a social statement – "I cannot work, I will not work, I will not/cannot exchange, HELP!" – and must be treated in a social context. As for overcoming the second obstacle, divulging information only if the listener has a relevant position, only one occasion arose I think, with Mr. Febvre. It implied an extreme relation of exchange, where there were no more limits to the flow of information: everything could and had to be said.

The normal situation of word exchange is one of vigilance and secrecy, and as Favret-Saada says, being *pris* means having a reason for talking. In La Brumaire in general, one must have reason not only to talk, but for almost everything one does. Sometimes when visiting, after a while I would be asked the question: "Is there something you came for?" (*Vous avez une commission?*), indicating to me that the reason for my visit was unclear (or, if the reason were clear, it did not in itself justify the visit). This mainly held for people who were not implicated in the land reallotment, but even those who were could demand an explanation if they thought I was visiting or asking too much – such a demand in itself was a way of stating just that: that I *was* doing "too much" of something. Likewise, people would never come to our house without having a valid reason, be it just a pretext like borrowing the phone or delivering something.

I have already talked about informational tugs-of-war, and as the naïve, innocent newcomer in these verbal tussles, I often fell victim to a deliberate "pulling worms out of the nose," as the French say. Again here, I was the one at fault, I was telling too much, "falling for it" and exhibiting lack of control. My interlocutors were visibly pleased by this, both because of the gratuitous news they obtained, and because I was so obviously not master of my words. They would shed their closed, secretive and protective demeanour and assume one of openness and confidence mixed with vigorous enjoyment. I gradually got better at detecting and resisting attempts to trap me into talking (I had good teachers), and eventually even came to master some of the tricks to make others take the plunge. I was thus able to test some of the limits of "too much" or "just enough" in a more controlled (albeit vicious) way than when I was the victim. My "teachers" (and potential victims) were always very pleased, even proud, when they caught me "tugging": I was getting better at controlling word-flow and thus becoming a worthier confidante and ally.

I mentioned the incident with the donkey foal, where I tried in vain to follow the emergence of a story; I never heard a word about it again, it was "too close." But on other occasions I became, or was assumed to be, the firsthand witness of affairs going on just around me. In those cases it became vital to make me talk, but since I had learned over time to master exchange and launch less willingly into free talking, I became the holder of potential exchange goods because I would only divulge something if I got something in return. Like my interlocutors, I was just as aware of and interested in the reflexive part, in testing out the exchange, as in the information itself. I got better at using the strategies that value potential knowledge, at simulating ignorance, keeping silent while my stock of information grew – in short, at managing information. As I got better, I also grew wiser on the subject overall. Had I remained passive, I would have encountered only silence, a silence with no meaning other than its own emptiness.

I think it was significant to the way people received me that I did not speak very correct French: enough to follow along and contribute, but not the never-ending stream of words that Parisians are known for. I also lacked precision, and encircled or evoked things rather than saying them directly, just like Brumairians do, although they do it on purpose, not because they cannot find the right words. My way of talking was apparently deemed appropriate, and although my lack of precision sometimes made me plunge in and say things I shouldn't have,[29] the fact that French was not my mother tongue was a plausible excuse. Unlike Herzfeld, who was defined as a foreigner and representative of a feared exterior power during the course of his fieldwork, partly, I presume, because of language (cf. Herzfeld 1983a), I think that my way of using French put me in an inferior position towards such exteriority, and on equal "linguistic terms" with other villagers.

A last brief comment as to *who* this process turned me into in relation to others: Favret-Saada became an interlocutor in discourse because she was supposedly *prise*, and I became an exchange partner for somewhat similar and somewhat different reasons. In both cases, we entered into orders of discourse and exchange on locally determined conditions; these discursive orders were also the field of our inquiry. We were not locals, but neither were we strangers. We were newcomers and became something else and something more over time – never locals, though. My purpose was to know about and to know how, but in that respect, I was no different from any other local inquirer, always on the lookout for knowledge and for knowledge about knowledge.

---

29 Like when I used the word *"crever"* (to burst, like a balloon or a tire) in reference to a person (*"Elle aurait pu en crever"*), while the expression in the local context is used figuratively only to describe animals as dead.
30 This corresponds to Bocage witchcraft, where the household is considered a whole, even if it is generally attacked through its individual members (Favret-Saada 1977).

Concluding Remarks on Exchange

When individuals exchange goods or deeds, they do so not only on their own behalf but on that of their immediate family or household. This is also generally the case when people exchange words. They represent the household as a whole.[30] Likewise, gifts are always given to the whole unit, never to individuals.

The exchange described here is one of equivalence and not of kind, and is based on time and durable contracts, and this complex of exchanges still seems to be classifiable under Mauss's definition of "total prestations" (1954: 3).

Some events, like giving and receiving blood sausage, distil and outline more distinctly the underlying principles of exchange and reciprocity: they are more "dense," to use Ardener's term, than the daily "stream of events" that they are a part of (1971a: 38; 1978: 90). And they seem to be dense not only to the person who studies how being becomes and who has anthropological terms at hand, but also to those locals who analyze village life without using such terms. Again, this is not to say that I became local, but to emphasize that the locals did just as much analyzing, "living" *and* "recording" (1978: 94) as I did, if not more.

Men have difficulty getting married these days, in La Brumaire as well as in most other parts of rural France. Women no longer accept the "non-status" of being a farmwife with no social security, no unemployment insurance and no professional pension but just as much work. This situation arises because according to administrative norms, most farms are too small to register two full-time farmers. The limited economic autonomy that women used to have by selling eggs, milk, cheese, chicken and so forth has disappeared with the emergence of E.E.C. regulations, and there are very few possibilities for finding local employment. Many young women prefer to ensure their autonomy by getting an education and a profession, which almost always means leaving the village. As a result, a large number of the farms of La Brumaire today are run by bachelors along with their siblings or aging parents. In Lévi-Straussian and Maussian terms, women have renounced being exchanged, the ultimate consequence of which is the disintegration of society. Even if Lévi-Strauss and Mauss prove to be wrong, if the undermining of this basic societal principle is not enough to extinguish the community, the fact that no children are being born is. "Total prestation" has its limits.

Despite the quest for discretion and silence, a whole lot of talking is going on in La Brumaire. Only rarely are words exchanged "uncharged" and void of information, although their "density" varies. If some words seem to be of no greater importance, the mere fact that they are being exchanged is significant. Moreover, the flow is not unregulated – on the contrary, it is highly controlled: nothing is said without reason or in return for nothing. Information is administered like a valuable, potential commodity for further exchange. Unlike goods and deeds that are immediately consumed, words, and the information they carry, endure and can be passed on. Somehow they even must be so, like necklaces in the Kula.

In a general manner, exchange in La Brumaire has undergone the evolution that Mauss describes in *The Gift*: an alienation of things and persons, the establishment of currency, and even dictated prices in most trade. Many Brumairians say that they "long for the days of their youth, when people were more helpful towards each other." Nevertheless, despite this apparent evolution and following the line of Mauss's analysis of exchange in modern society, exchange and reciprocity still seem to be at the basis of common life in the village, and the lamenting of ancient times and traditions only reinforces the principle. As was so eloquently said about a couple who did not engage in exchange of any kind, not even a "hello" to the postman: "They are in the void" (*Ils sont dans le néant*). I hardly think the social significance of exchange can be made more manifest.

When people say they long for the generosity of their youth, it is probably more an expression of the ambiguous or paradoxical relation of exchange between an ideal reciprocity on one side and inequality and withholding on the other – an atemporal ideal of interpersonal balance existing in the present, changed to an evolution in their minds – than it is the reflection of an actual, historical evolution.[31] In some exchanges

---

31 Assuming that it has always been like that, and that nostalgia could actually be defined as the transposition of present paradoxes or ambiguities into the past and the time dimension, then the atemporality or synchrony is diachronous.

like that of blood sausage, reciprocity is scrupulously maintained. In others like word exchange, inequality – getting more than one gives – is sought outright. Furthermore, as we have seen, people do not share everything, and inequity in the economic potential of different persons and households persists. It seems as if the eternal fear of the jealousy of neighbours and their interference with one's "vital force" expressed in accusations of witchcraft and in its parallel discourses is precisely the result of a confrontation of these two opposites, reciprocity and inequality. Witches and jealous neighbours have not received their just due; they (that is, the discourses about them) express the antithesis of reciprocating.

4

Spying

4.1 Countryside Semiotics

When Brumairians (and people in general for that matter) move around in the landscape, they are, and leave, traces; they traverse and transform it. They "write" with their movements, and like the ephemeral design cut by skaters in the surface of ice, their movements and traces construct an ever-changing text, "*écrit*" in the landscape[1] – an "*écrit*" that is public and social, for movements and traces are interpreted as signs of actions. As de Certeau says, movements transform a potential place (*lieu*) into a space (*espace*); space is practised place (1990: 173),[2] like a chessboard that comes alive through the moves of its players, the motion of its pieces. People's movements write meaning into place, transforming it into a social space or landscape.

All texts come alive only through their readers; as we saw with the words in magic books, they are only potentially powerful and must be pronounced to become socially efficient. In the same way, movements and their traces in the landscape take on meaning because they are constantly being read and interpreted by the people who inhabit and practise it. The writing and reading of movements are simultaneous whereas traces are read at a moment other than that of writing, as is the case with books; there is diachrony, and the time lapse is part of the trace.

If people's movements and traces are said to be read and interpreted, it implies that such movements and traces say something about something else, that they are signs. This is indeed the way Brumairians consider the attention paid to what goes on in the landscape: all actions and their eventual traces are interpreted as signs of something else. Making interpretation part of Brumairian sign-use implies that there is no sign without a reader, that signs say something about something else to *someone*.

---

1 "Text" seems qualified by the permanency of printing whereas "*écrit*" (literally, "written" or "writing") is associated with movement, like casually written notes or the ephemeral design of ice-skaters. "Text" and "*écrit*" suggest that everyday life is communication with senders and receivers.
2 An English edition of this work exists as *The Practice of Everyday Life,* transl. by S. Rendall, Berkeley: University of California Press, 1984. However, I have chosen to cite and translate excerpts from the French edition.

Before undertaking a closer description of sign-use in La Brumaire, it would be appropriate to establish what kind of signs we are dealing with, what the nature of the meaning they contain and convey is, and in what way they can be included in or connected to an overall idea of semiotics. It is not my intention to apply a readymade theoretical complex to Brumairian signs because they in themselves give many clues as to their nature and the ways in which they function. But since we are dealing with something that looks and seemingly behaves like signs, and since people, including myself, use the word "signs" to refer to them, and since semiotics seems to be a very inclusive and permissive term dealing with a large range of communication, meaning, codes, and sign production, the concept and practice of spying seems to inscribe itself – naturally in this wide theoretical complex.

A Preliminary Sign-Experience and Some General Ideas about Signs

In order to discuss the nature of some of the signs involved here and the relationships linking form to content, let us take an example: From the flow of sound that constantly meets the ear when one is standing in the middle of a landscape, one might be able to distinguish specific sounds, like the roar of a chainsaw or the bellow of a cow, by more or less unconsciously analyzing such acoustic parameters as pitch, timbre, dynamics and rhythm. Identifying a specific sound like that of a chainsaw can, alone or combined with other parameters, for example spatial and temporal ones, enable one to guess or even determine what chainsaw is being used, where, and maybe by whom. One might be able to hear whether trees are being felled, maybe even what kind of tree, or whether wood is being cut up, and eventually, how much. If voices are heard from the same direction, one might be able to assume that several persons are working together and also, if the signal is clear enough, determine who they are. In each case, the degree of substitution or interpretation depends on the alignment of received information with former experience. The picnicking tourist might not know the difference between the sound of a chainsaw and a motocross bike, let alone the specific sound that Jean-Pierre's old Yamaha emits when felling half-rotten oak.

So according to the degree of interpretation, more or less information or meaning can be extracted from the experience of hearing the sound of the chainsaw coupled with its spatial parameters. For example, "Someone is cutting trees," versus "Jean-Pierre is finally cutting that old oak that was so dangerously hanging over the road," or "René and Jean-Pierre are on good terms again, since René is using Jean-Pierre's chainsaw," or "Jean-Pierre's chainsaw needs oil," and so on. "Someone is riding around on a motocross bike" is of course yet another interpretation.

Identification
Before going any further, it would be interesting to determine whether the sound of a chainsaw can be considered a sign in some semiotic sense. The answer, of course, depends on whom we ask. First of all, the acoustic signal coming to the ear of a person is usually interpreted as more than just the sound of a chainsaw (which in itself already links the sound to a signified). In that sense, the sound is a representation, "something standing for something else" (Eco 1976: 16), implying a relationship between a physical component (visual, audible, olfactory, etc.) and its meaning: thus the sound is a sign. Eco adds that "In culture, any entity becomes a semiotic phenomenon" (Eco 1973: 71). In an equally generous manner, Barthes considers all objects, ranging from hats to gestures, texts and symphonies, to be signs that have a sense, a meaning (even when they seem meaningless, for then *that* is their meaning) (Barthes 1985: 258). It therefore seems plausible to conceive of the sound of a chainsaw as a semiotic sign.

Another criterion under discussion is that of intention. Saussure's definition of signs implies intentional, artificial communication, which in theory rules out a whole range of unintentional sign-making of the order of some of those studied in La Brumaire. According to Eco,

> those who share Saussure's notion of semiology distinguish sharply between intentional, artificial devices (which they call 'signs') and other natural or unintentional manifestations which do not, strictly speaking, deserve such a name. (Eco 1976: 15)

But the question is in what way such distinctions are relevant here. If we return to the example of the chainsaw, although René's main

They're heating the back room. "Armand must be ill again."
                                                                 "*Dumas has been drinking.*"

intention might be to cut wood, he is very well aware that the sound of Jean-Pierre's chainsaw coming from his farm will be interpreted as a sign of their renewed good relationship. So although the social statement would probably be designed more as an "unintentional manifestation" in Saussurian terms, it is still part of, and cannot be dissociated from, the intentional sign-act of cutting wood. And, more generally, although sign-emission is sometimes unintentional or even unwanted, it is never unconscious. People always know when they are emitting signs, and they are just as good at registering their own signs as others – with the modification, of course, that even if people always know they are emitting and are aware of the variety of possible interpretations, ultimately they cannot know the actual content of those various readings.

Conversely, Peirce's definition of a sign, adopted by Eco, only confirms the semiotic nature of Brumairian signs, for it does not require intention. To Saussure's binary sign definition, Peirce adds a third element, namely the interpreting subject: a sign is "something which stands for something *to* somebody" (ibid.; italics mine). That interpretation prevails over sign-production in our definition also renders the distinction between "natural" and "artificial" signs irrelevant. The slight humidity on a rock, an indication of approaching rain, is just as meaningful a sign to those who know how to read it as the bellow of a cow or a stop sign at an intersection are.[3]

Finally, Eco prefers to speak of "sign-functions" rather than signs, the sign-function being the correlation of expression and content. Each time a given expression is correlated to another content, there is a new sign-function (for example when the same word has different meanings) (ibid.).

Up to now, what we have is a sign that is perceptible to the senses, that may be artificial or natural, that is not always intentionally emitted, that depends on a potential interpreter who might also be the emitter, and that may convey different meanings to different interpreters. The essential thing here is that there be translation, interpretation.

---

3 I purposely use the loud bellow of a hungry cow, certainly intentional communication, as an example of an artificial sign to illustrate that the distinctions are not clear in the first place.

Degree of Interpretation
Obviously, a sign or a signal cannot be seen in isolation from its meanings. It is the total "sign-function," the actual interpretations of specific signs, that interest us, not the signs alone, for ultimately if there is no interpretation, there is no sign.

But as we have seen, the same sound, the same sign may represent a wide variety of different contents. According to what I have called the degree of substitution or interpretation, the sound of the chainsaw can be interpreted as for example "|rrrrr| = 'motocross bike'" (which is false, but that does not affect the sign) or "|rrrrr| = 're-established social relation'" (which might also be a misinterpretation for that matter). So what is the relationship between the different meanings that can be construed from the same sign? And what are the implications of signs having several different meanings?

First of all, it is clear that we cannot attribute a primary meaning to the sound of the chainsaw. When it comes to words and their lexicon, it is usually possible to indicate a certain word's denotation even if it changes with time and context, but in semiotics in general there exists no dictionary assigning a primary, denotative meaning to signs. And since from an analytical point of view we are interested in social significance and not primary meanings, nor in distinguishing between true and false versions (Is it a chainsaw or a motocross bike?), there is no need to distinguish between denotation and connotation. There is no one, true interpretation. In fact we could say that everything is connotation, and all interpretations are equally valid. "Degree" should therefore not be understood as a measure of exactitude but as an expression of the variety of different meanings of a sign.

This implication is linked to a second problem, namely that in Peirce's definition, signs are defined by their form alone. The only variable is the sign itself, the form; but the meaning of a given sign is fixed. So even if Peirce includes the interpreter in the sign-definition, his distinction is nevertheless based on this unique relation between sign and content, and therefore on a singular and somewhat abstract interpreter. But as we see with the example of the chainsaw, the same sign represents a wide variety of different contents according to its relation to other signs and sign-elements, spatial and temporal parameters, and to its different interpreters.

It follows that to deal with signs in La Brumaire, we must necessarily add the factor of a multitude of interpreters, and thus meanings, to Peirce's definition. For within a social and discursive context, what interests us is the variety and difference of meanings with which every single sign can be vested. We cannot think of signs and their interpretation without thinking of a community of particular interpreters.

The interpreting of the sound of the chainsaw in different ways necessarily has to do with the specific interpreters and their individual knowledge and experience. We end up with a sign-relation that is quite relative and uncertain, and which corresponds very well to the ambiguity and reversibility of utterances that we encountered earlier. In this respect, when people are discussing the implications of a certain action, or when they tell the same story in different versions, they are proposing different interpretations of the same sign; they are negotiating its content. In this discursive field nothing is ever certain, there is no one denotative sense of a sign, no built-in "true" interpretation. All signs remain inconstant and open to negotiation.

Seen from this perspective, we can conceive of talking and stories as collective reinterpretations of the relationship between signs and their meaning(s) based on the mutual exchange of individual experience and knowledge.

Significance
To some, the unevenness of the rows of wheat in the field to the left of the intersection at La Braire is a sign – and a confirmation – of the incestuous relation between the owner's mother and her brother. To others, it is a sign of drunkenness; to still others, it is not a sign of anything and thus not a sign at all, for there is no interpretation, no interpreter (although Barthes might say it was a sign of its own insignificance...). But as we have seen, the emitter – in this case, the peasant who let his tractor swerve a little when he was sowing wheat – is usually the first interpreter. He is guided by the same sense of significance as other interpreters, although he may not deduce the same meaning.

Among the interpreters of the unevenness of the rows of wheat, a few might deduce that the driver of the tractor was drunk while sowing, a few will probably deduce other meanings, like general negligence or lack of experience, while most will tend to correlate the sign with supposed incest: if he is inept it is because his biological parents were brother and sister.

This is of course a theoretical construction for which I have no figures, but the point is only made to demonstrate the following: even if a sign can be interpreted in a variety of possible ways, not all interpretations are equally probable. It is very unlikely, for example, that uneven rows of wheat would be interpreted as proof of the existence of God or a sign of approaching rain. Nothing should be excluded of course, since we depend on our interpreters to extract meaning, and potentially their number is infinite and their reasoning without limits. But nevertheless, since they all base their interpretations on knowledge and prior experience, and because knowledge and experience are something collectively exchanged and shared, thereby structuring further interpretation, some meanings impose themselves before others. They seem to order themselves around what we could call a centre of social significance; a centre that should not be confused with the truth however.

For the picnicking tourist, it is not important whether René and Jean-Pierre are on good terms again, but that peace and quiet is being spoiled, either by a motocross bike or by a chainsaw. For René's brother, Claude, on the other hand, supposing that he can count on Jean-Pierre's help again for harvesting instead of having to ask his neighbour for help is almost vital. In this sense, it is the interpreters – our community of interpreters – who get our primary analytical attention, or in other words, who encompass the sign.

Dimensions
According to the above definitions, signs can be of various dimensions and constellations, incorporated in action (including speech), in the traces left by such action, and sometimes constructed into whole sign complexes. Later I will discuss these different sign-forms as movements, traces and surfaces.

Objects can constitute signs insofar as they say something else to someone, and so can constellations of several objects, almost always combined with spatial parameters. An object in one place can mean something different than the same object in another place; an animal trace pointing in a certain direction means something specific about its movements; few objects, if any at all, mean something in isolation, and furthermore never exist as such.

Humans by their very presence can be signs in the same way as objects. A person doing something or going somewhere can be a sign, and so can speech and silence, as we have seen. Such signs belong to the domain of action or movements.

Graves erected in a pattern (a cemetery), constitute an *écrit*, a sign surface, as do fields patched together into a landscape. The simple fact that the word, "graveyard," correlates with the actual graveyard, identifies it as a unit; conversely, the physical graveyard comes to "stand for," among other things, the word.

4.2 *Local Detectives: Seeing, Hearing, Smelling*

– "So how was the film?"
– "???"
– "Well, yesterday when I passed your house at 8:00 p.m., Mme. P. had parked the car, and this morning I could see that one of you had been out driving in the meantime."
– "??"
– "You always park the car slightly slanted, she never does. You went to La Châtre, judging from the angle. And where else can you go there after 8:00, except to the cinema?"

The signs springing up, inhabiting and shaping the Brumairian landscape could be described three ways: as movements, traces, and surfaces. A car passing by (movement), the regular rows of a newly sown field (trace), the pattern of fields and meadows delimited by hedges, creeks, barbed wire and roads (surface): all this is part of daily Brumairian sign production and interpretation.

The signs involved are mainly visible and audible, and as we have seen in the stories, sometimes olfactory; taste and touch are also employed. Our local detectives use all senses. Traces are mainly visible and olfactory, while movements are mainly visible and audible (for sound is movement, oscillation); surfaces are all three (five). Words, phrases, stories, talking and silence are all part of the general complex of signs.

Signs in the Landscape: Movements, Traces, Surfaces

Describing signs... How can I provide solid data for a description that is so much based on intuition, sensing, seeing, listening, smelling, and on what goes on in the minds of people, where those sensations are transformed into meaning? I can describe signs physically, but as far as their interpretation and meaning are concerned, I can only give an impression, a kind of "language shadow" as Ardener says, of something that is much more and involves all senses – something that is never really articulated, but which stems from experiences I had, like walking in the meadows and feeling that every tree had eyes (a sensation that grew over time as my knowledge of spying expanded and my movements became more significant to others); from people deliberately or inadvertently revealing how they came to know about other peoples' doings; from taking part in spying and interpreting movements and traces. For, notwithstanding that people are well aware of their own and others' spying and analyzing, no one ever told me how signs were interpreted except on very rare occasions, like when Collet revealed his analysis of our car parking, or corrected our careless trace-leaving which gave us away, not only to him but to others. Otherwise, I just had to be on the lookout like everyone else, relying on my local teachers; for I spied on spying like they did.

Movements
Birds moving, bodies moving, vehicles moving, vibrations making sound (vocal cords, machine parts, wind, church bells, footsteps).

When dusk falls, curtains are drawn, shutters shut, and everyone withdraws into their homes. Outside, there is emptiness, except for the occasional car or stray dog. Retreat, enclosure, the public sphere ceases to exist – or so it seems. For behind these apparently closed and slumbering façades, people are still wide awake, on the lookout,[4] registering everything: sounds near and far, movements, bypassers, all signs are detected. Cars are distinguished by their sound, and if unknown, identified as such. Their direction, speed, eventual halts, are detected. Detected likewise are doors being opened or shut, voices emanating from neighbouring houses, footsteps, cows lowing or moving restlessly, dogs barking. Lucienne always knows when we have arrived; she may go to bed at nine, but she hears us even when we pass by after midnight.

When the sun comes up and people are out in the open, eyes become just as vigilant as ears were in the dark. Only twenty or thirty years ago, many people moved around by foot, but today they pass by quickly in a car, so great attention is paid to cars: who has what car – the model and colour, even the license number, how it sounds when running, when stopped, when the doors close, etc. – and who has changed cars recently. Moving people are now mainly identified by their cars. Licence plates indicating what region the car is from are scrutinized – "23, *un*

---

4 "*Sur le qui-vive,*" on the alert as to "who's alive, who's out there."

marchois": someone from La Creuse, the next department to the south. Conversations tone down when a car passes, and all eyes discreetly follow the bypasser's trail. Attention to cars has to do with knowing who goes where, to see whom: obviously, this is one of the more important things to know.

Some transportation could be avoided by telephoning, because a lot of visiting is done simply to deliver messages. But telephoning is avoided, probably not only because it demands a more direct kind of speech, but also because telephoning carries with it no public statement, and no inscription in the landscape.

Reading others' movements is necessary to knowing, but writing with movements is necessary to inscribe oneself in the social, to express allegiance, and ultimately to exist; and for this, one depends on readings and interpretations of others. Working together, going to a funeral, attending a village feast, sitting at specific tables and drinking together, buying in one shop and not another, are all important public signs bearing witness to the state of one's current social field of tension. There is word that the members of the reallotment commission have come to acute disagreement, but we don't know for sure. "We'll see at the silage." Who comes, who helps whom, no clearer answer can be given.

Other types of movements of equal eloquence:

– Charles's cows are running wild again; he just can't manage to fix a fence.

– The storks are going south, and winter is coming.

Traces
Footprints, parked cars, fields, animals, the current state of things.

Cars parked in certain places, certain ways, hints as to who is where and for how long, who has been driving, and eventually, in what state of drunkenness. An old car, well tended, a sign of care, diligent work and thrift. A flashy new car, an open sign of wealth and excessive spending.

Nice straight rows of newly sown wheat and corn, a sign of skill and carefulness, of good work. Uneven rows, a waste of space, poor work, *"petit travail."* A young man swerved a little with the tractor when sowing wheat and his father is very upset: "It'll look like that for months, and it's right next to the road where everyone can see it!"

"So Lucienne has been visiting Durand...?"
　　　　　　　　"Lefevre is helping old Labaye bring in the hay!"

Animals in the field, their species, size, condition and quantity, the state of the harvest, how dense, how high, how many weeds, whether fences are maintained and the hedges trimmed, whether the trees are well pruned, whether there are dead ones, whether weed-killer has been used – all are traces and testimonials of the owners' working abilities.

Light in the windows, smoke from the chimney: someone is home. Light out front, someone is visiting or visitors are expected. "Don't turn the lights on. They'll see you have visitors" ("*N'allumez pas, ils veront qu'il y a du monde*").

Door and shutters open all day in all seasons meaning that one is home, one can receive. When closed, something is wrong, someone is dead. Marceau is ill and dying, many cars are parked outside, they are watching over him; but the shutters are still open, so all is well.

Curtains moving; someone has been looking out, spying too openly. The texture of curtains, thin, thick, transparent. Jeanne shows me her new curtains. She is not satisfied: they are too thin and she sees everything, which was not the purpose. But had they been thicker, more opaque, it would be a sign she wasn't interested in spying out, in taking part in village life, and moreover, people might think she had something to hide. So, all in all... Jeanne's curtains show how the frontier between inside and outside, between public and private, are sensitive and difficult to manage. The curtains' relative transparency leaves a necessary passage open between two apparently exclusive spheres, permits communication, exchange. And finally, Jeanne will never find the perfect curtains, for there is no perfect balance, no definitive mediation.

Closed shutters, the occupants have withdrawn for the evening, severing their view to and their visibility from the outside world. Only that strange new family down the road leaves their shutters open all night: one can, one almost must, see right into their illuminated living room, how very unpleasant. Just as odour can be contagious to sensible passersby, making them complicit to crime by promoting their open knowledge of it, light and images shed so promiscuously upon passing eyes oblige them to see, and ultimately know. Like nakedness: it is attractive, but one hardly wants to be witness to it out in the open street. It is more offensive to the eye that sees publicly than to the skin that is seen publicly.

Nature's traces. All those chestnut trees in the hedge, they grow abundantly only where the soil is very rich. And the weather: it is still dry, but the rocks are moist, there will soon be rain.

Surfaces
Movements and traces, an arbitrary distinction, not made by Brumairians. Movements and traces form patterns of signs of the same type, like texts on a specialized topic, and these patterns, full of social manifestations, I call surfaces: landscapes, cemeteries, maps, webs of high-tension cables, TGV-tracks. They could be characterized as systems of signs, based on difference, opposition, contrast (cf. Barthes 1966).

The cemetery, a highly social space, lies open to the curious reader. The cemetery is like a small-scale copy of society, with little buildings, housing souls, on delimited space. The whole village, its former and current inhabitants are there, if not yet physically, then as a space reserved. Their tombstones are them, stand for them. Some graves are rich marble edifices with figurines and golden inscriptions, others plain rock. Like the land and houses, they must be tended to. And like investing in land, investing in a new stone for the family grave is a sign of reason. It is as if the cemetery should be kept updated, reflecting the current state of village affairs. When one comes into money, one buys land – and a new tombstone.

As the cemetery represents the occupation of village space, it also presents time. The names and dates on the tombstones and the length of the lists show the depth of anchorage in village soil. The Deguet's have been here for centuries, the Delong's have just arrived. It shows former alliances consolidated by marriage, since women are also mentioned with their maiden names. ...Oh, so old Auchamp's mother was actually a Pichet girl! Today the two families don't get along at all, something must have happened... The extent to which a name appears in the cemetery shows the importance of that family at a specific period, or in general. Some families have died out and have no more living descendants, others show their potential by having grown bigger, occupying more cemetery and village soil. Some tombstones can even testify to unhappy family histories with many premature dead, others to long family lives undisturbed.

Some have...

Some don't.

The cemetery is a valuable surface for he or she who knows how to read it. Insight into village affairs is necessary to get its full potential, and village and cemetery enlighten one another. But like any representation, the relation between them, between village social order and cemetery, is not just one-to-one. Both have their internal logic, their own modes of expression, and an element in one is not necessarily translatable into an element in the other. When one wealthy old bachelor died, there was disagreement as to which grave to put him in. Actually he belonged with his parents, but his distant niece, as if to reinforce the claims she made to the inheritance, managed under some vague pretext to get him buried in her family grave. Thus, people's positions are negotiable even after death. But once they're in the ground, they're in to stay. The irreversibility of one's position once one is dead and buried does not reflect living life. Choosing sides while alive is reversible, but once dead, one can only be buried in a single grave, and cannot change camps thereafter. Still, if who's where in the cemetery does not reflect the distribution of village space completely accurately, it nevertheless gives clues to the matters of conflict and power.

Landscape
I doubt whether there is any profession whatsoever where, to the same extent as for the farmer, one's working ability (or potency) literally lies open for all to see, like the pages of a gradebook. Every hedge and ditch, every stalk of wheat is the result and reflection of the farmer's invested aptitudes. The animals are still inside, the animals are already out, they have strayed again, they look skinny, they look fat and healthy, they have few calves this year. The hay looks good, his tractor needs repairing, the rows are uneven, the family has a big vegetable garden this year, the hedges are well trimmed, he's chopped lots of wood... Naturally we can count on our Brumairian detectives to read this open source of knowledge down to the last detail, and to draw their conclusions.

Actually, a trip through the countryside is a voyage through the current social order. It is like attending a fashionable party, where the hostess takes you around and introduces everyone by name and profession, except that in the fields you rarely ever meet anyone. Instead, you get acquainted with something more than a person's bodily

"Oh, Brigand's had his harvester repaired, must have cost a fortune..."
"Marcelle's sheep look very healthy this year."

expression, you become acquainted with the foundations of their being, namely their working potency ("X can") and their potential ("X has"). As François and Lucienne go driving, they "read" and discuss:

> – That's young Brelot, he sowed corn this year. – He should trim the hedge. – And there's Mme. Picard, she's at the clinic, isn't she? – Yes, she rented it to Faugère. He put his cows there, they're looking good, eh? – And that's Faucher... It's a big field, eh? And very good. The apple trees yield a lot too. Hey, Marcel's letting his hay rot. – Yes, but you know, his wife is sick. – But Lucien could harvest it, couldn't he? – Well, they're not getting along at the moment, since René broke his tractor. – And there, look, Menard dredged his stream, now his cows will fall in. – That's because he always listens to Laurain. – And there, that's Roger Meillant, you know, who...5

This narrative journey through the landscape brings to mind de Certeau's words linking space and story:

> Every story is the account of a voyage – a practice of space. ...These narrated adventures, which produce geographies of action and at the same time float in the common places of an order, do not just constitute a "supplement" to pedestrian enunciations and progression rhetoric. They do more than displace and transpose these into the field of language. In fact, they organize the steps. They make the journey before or while the feet carry it out. (de Certeau 1990: 171)[6]

It is not only the voyage that creates the *récits*, or stories, but also the stories that organize the voyage. While reading the landscape, people

---

5 "– Ça, c'est le petit Brelot, il a mis du maïs cette année. – Il devrait tailler la bouchure. – Et là, c'est Mme. Picard, elle est à la clinique, non ? – Si, elle l'a loué à Faugère. Il a mis ses vaches... elles sont belles, hein. – Et ça, c'est Faucher... c'est un grand champ, hein. Et très bon. Les pommiers donnent bien aussi. Tien, Marcel laisse pourrir son foin. – Oui, mais tu sais, sa femme est malade. – Mais Lucien pourrait le rentrer, non ? – Ben, ils sont pas très bien en ce moment, tu sais, avec René qui a cassé son tracteur. – Et là – tiens, Menard a récuré son ruisseau, les vaches vont tomber dedans. – Ça, c'est parce qu'il écoute toujours ce que lui dit Laurain. – Et là, c'est Roger Meillant, tu sais, qui a..."

6 "Tout récit est un récit de voyage, – une pratique de l'espace... Ces aventures narrées, qui tout à la fois produisent des géographies d'actions et dérivent dans les lieux communs d'un ordre, ne constituent pas seulement un « supplément » aux énonciations piétonnières et aux rhétoriques cheminatoires. Elles ne se contentent pas de les déplacer et transposer dans le champ du langage. En fait, elles organisent les marches. Elles font le voyage, avant ou pendant que les pieds l'exécutent."

are at the same time investing it with stories already told. The landscape has no gaps, no uninvested, "virgin" land. All space is occupied and marked by an owner. But like the cemetery, there is no singular relationship between spatial and social order. Some people do not own land, are not like others embedded in the landscape. These people most often come from tenant families who have always worked for and been housed by others, and have never had the opportunity to buy property of their own. The fact that they have no land of course is a sign of their spatial insignificance, but is not in itself spatial. And land counts for much, but not everything. So the spatial says something – but not everything – about the social, and vice versa.

Another surface, this one authoritative, is the cartographic representation of the landscape. The local conception of the landscape corresponds to the way it is practised, in time and space, as daily movements (cf. de Certeau 1990: 170-91). This conflicts with the landscape as seen through the eye of land reallotment surveyors and reflected in their maps. De Certeau talks very precisely of

> the relationship between the itinerary (a discursive series of operations) and the map (a totalizing flattening of observations), that is, between two symbolic and anthropological languages of space. Two poles of experience. (ibid.: 176)[7]

Many Brumairians acted in accordance with this distinction: to find their way around the maps of the surveyor, they would start by finding their own house, and then using their finger, they would depart from there, as they did every day on their feet in the landscape. They could not conceive of their property, nor that of their neighbours for that matter, as anything other than an itinerary, because that was how they experienced it. This incongruity between conflicting experiences of the landscape was characteristic of the whole problem posed by the land reallotment, which opposed two completely different domains of discourse and experience, one belonging to the authorities and the other to the locals, neither of whom were ever really able to understand each other.

---

7 "...la relation entre l'itinéraire (une série discursive d'opérations) et la carte (une mise à plat totalisant des observations), c'est à dire entre deux langages symboliques et anthropologiques de l'espace. Deux pôles de l'expérience."

Itinerary, finding one's way: "You pass this gate and go down the track..."
   Map: a flattening juxtaposition, the surveyor's view, unexperienced.

Discord not only arose when people consulted the maps posted in the town hall, but was articulated directly in the landscape, where the vision and divisions of the surveyors, marked by fluorescent orange landmarks, were imposed over the landscape in its actual, locally created and practised form. Where there was a hedge full of well tended apple- and plum-trees, the surveyor programmed fields; where there was a meadow with a small reservoir, the surveyor programmed ditches; where there was wheat, the surveyor programmed barbed-wire fences. The existing, practised space contrasted with a virtual distribution that was, as it turned out, inevitably realized in the end. If the little orange landmarks could be characterized as symbolic power reproducing political and economic power in an unrecognizable form (cf. Bourdieu 1977), they were certainly not very well disguised. Brumairians certainly did recognize and read the landmarks as the imposition of external powers on internal village affairs. Perhaps such landmarks were not symbols masking an underlying distribution of power that was truer, more "real"; perhaps both landmarks and the external power symbolized in them were in some way masks or reflections of each other – different ways of saying the same thing.

Another more "infrastructural" surface within the landscape is the web composed of high-tension cables, gas pipes, highways and TGV-tracks. Running through without stopping here, high-tension cables bring electricity to distant towns from a big power station west of the commune, and huge subterranean gas-pipes, indicated by large yellow marker-boards in the fields and hedges, transport gas from somewhere far away to other unknown places. Electricity pilons and cables, and gas-pipe markers are there in the landscape, reminders of the remoteness and unimportance of places they traverse but never supply. People in La Brumaire get their gas in cannisters. The *TGV* (high-speed train) with its special tracks, incompatible with normal trains, has been projected to run through La Brumaire and the hamlets of La Forêt and Brunoy. But it is still questionable whether it will stop at Chateauroux, the department's capital; otherwise it will just run non-stop from Orléans to Limoges, bringing coffee-drinking, magazine-reading passengers through La Forêt at 470 kilometres per hour.

A highway is under construction in some of the neighbouring communes, and similar to the TGV, will not be accessible from the smaller

Signs in the fields, reminders of remoteness...

Commodities just passing through.

roads around it, only from the major towns where it connects with other highways. Small tunnels are being made under it so locals (and rabbits) will still get their mail, and by making a detour can tend to the other half of their fields, family and friends. It is not that Brumairians expect a TGV station or a highway off-ramp in La Brumaire: these would not be used, for Brumairians don't do business in Limoges or Orléans. But all these infrastructural artefacts, like stripes from a jet in the sky, bear witness to local people's distance from the centres of decision-making, their relative unimportance and, to use another of Ardener's terms, their remoteness (Ardener 1987).

Gas-pipes or high-tension cables might easily be interpreted as signs of importance and modernity, but villagers have simply to remember the way they were installed there: the uniformed representative from the electric company formally asked landowners if they agreed to having the huge poles in their fields, but he also said if they didn't, the poles would be planted anyway. When the gas-pipes were installed and their big yellow indicators planted on the land, landowners were not even consulted, for technically, they only have surface rights.

Some final remarks about a special element of sign-surfaces, namely frontiers, and about the relativism of signs – remarks that may be banal, but that have been taken somewhat for granted until now:

The landscape is constructed of signs that are identifiable as units insofar as they say something to someone about something else. A field is a delimited unit, a sign of something else: in the most overall sense, of a person, its owner/user. And the hedges and ditches that delimit a field from a neighbouring one also demarcate and differentiate the owner from the neighbour, reflecting their respective potency and potential. As Barthes says, objects, in his very broad sense of the term, signify by their difference, their contrast to other objects (Barthes 1966: 250). Fields are signs only insofar as they are delimited from each other by frontiers. These delimiters, also signs in themselves, are points of both mutuality and differentiation between neighbours (cf. de Certeau 1990: 186).

Each sign acquires its meaning through its differentiation from others. If Pignon's field is large ("Pignon has, Pignon can"), it is only large in comparison to the other fields around it ("Deguet can't, hasn't as much"). To the north, in the Champagne Berrichonne, Pignon's field would be considered extremely small. Likewise, the tombstones in the

"Etienne is a hardworking guy, a good cultivateur.
But Henri just lets nature take over."

cemetery at La Brumaire find expression in their relationship to others around them. Yet overall, the cemetery looks rather poor compared to the cemetery of La Châtre for example, where the tombstones are bigger and more extravagant. The two graveyards say something general about the relationship between the inhabitants of the two villages – as do the small local fields compared to the larger ones of the Champagne – and they are also interpreted this way.

Some Significant Personalities

Up to this point, we have been observing mostly how spies make sense of what they experience, and less how they go about seeing, hearing and smelling – the basics of spying. Spying can be exemplified by some key figures. Ordinary people spy very well during their day-to-day activities and movements (which are themselves subject to spying). But some people are even more fortunate because their occupations afford them better possibilities for legitimately getting around, getting to know things and arriving unexpectedly.

The postman is one of those ambiguous figures who provoke both joy and anxiety. No one is talked about with so much suspicion as the two main postmen of La Brumaire; some people even express overt hostility towards theirs. People always seem to be either on very good or very bad terms with him; either way, they are still cautious and uneasy, for the postman always has a pretext for coming in. He arrives without notice, steps into one's privacy, and even if you do not invite him in for a glass of wine or a coffee, he nevertheless gets a thorough glance at your house and courtyard every morning. If he has a parcel, he comes right up to the door, again without notice. To prevent him from seeing in or entering would, like heavy curtains, be a sign one had something to hide. So he crosses these boundaries, and as a result he knows about what is going on around you.

Negotiating a relationship with him is an intricate matter, like selecting curtains, for he is by definition *en route*, a public functionary legitimately going from one private sphere to another. He knows something about the place he just came from, and shortly he'll proceed to the next household to deliver the letters and possibly the newly acquired secrets. If one can remain on good terms with him, the scales might tip slightly in one's favour, permitting one to get more information from him than he passes on to others. But at the same time he is not just a neutral channel of information, he is himself involved in local conflicts and alliance groups, and hence cannot always be on good terms with everyone. His very presence within one's private sphere is somehow conspicuous, easily interpreted as a sign he might be doing more there than merely performing his official function.

Conversely, for the postman himself, the obligatory trespassing of boundaries and relatively easy access to private knowledge is not an unequivocal advantage. As we saw earlier, there are things that people prefer not to know about others, because knowing somehow makes knowers accomplices. The postman is also a perfect scapegoat for accusations of leaking and spreading gossip, and he must go about handling his information carefully, so as not to be suspected of being a conniving "flatterer" (*flatteur*) or a "tattler" (*pipelette*). If he tells "too much" at one place, he is likely to do the same elsewhere. The role of the postman is a powerful one, but it can be turned against him, just as a sorcerer can suddenly be accused of bewitching instead of unwitching, of reading books and knowing too much. Furthermore, just as his presence can compromise the people he visits if he enters their house or stays too long (to deliver a parcel or obtain a signature, for instance), it can also compromise himself, especially when that someone is not his ally. For ultimately only his actions account for who his allies are...

One of the postmen in La Brumaire is a village Councillor. His daily routine alone probably constituted a perfect election campaign: his customers wanted to accommodate him to be on good terms with him. But during the reallotment conflict and because of his Council seat which gave him both knowledge and responsibility, he had serious problems negotiating his relations as many of his former ally households either rejected him or tried to get information out of him. He took a long sick-leave and threatened to resign from either his Council seat or his job.

The position of postman is indeed a delicate one. It shows that knowledge and knowing has its limits, not so much in a quantitative sense (knowing "too much") for ultimately that is not possible, but again, in the qualitative sense of knowing "too obviously."

Another key figure is the veterinarian, who comes less often than the postman, but who enters into the hearth-and-home of the families he visits, tending to their "vital force," to put it in Favret-Saada's terms (1977). He is called only when there are serious problems with the livestock, and raising livestock is the main livelihood around La Brumaire. It is probably no coincidence that the local veterinarian is also a local Mayor. Furthermore, his brother runs the only pharmacy and thus knows all about people's health. As someone said about the vet's political influence, "Imagine, they own the pharmacy and he's the veterinarian. He sees (knows) everything."[8] Furthermore, as I said elsewhere, this particular vet is familiar with ideas about supernaturally induced disease, stating that people often suggest that the illnesses he's called upon to cure are caused by sorcery, meaning that people consider his knowledge of local affairs sufficient to deal with the social dimensions of the problem.

In addition to these two figures, the two village merchants also go around delivering from house to house, enjoying a chat here and a chat there. They do announce their arrival by honking their horn before driving up in front, giving people a chance to hide whatever it is they have to hide. Nevertheless, the merchants obviously help news get around quite a lot quicker as well.

Another albeit rare figure is the census-taker who visits all the households every four or five years to gather demographic information for the national census. Notably, he or she is always a local who, with a long list of questions about the occupants of the household, gets very accurate information about age, former and current occupations, and legal data concerning the relations between the occupants and the distribution of responsibilities – all information that, normally, is not freely revealed to anyone outside the household. Even if *recenseurs* are bound by law not to divulge what they know, it is still a fact that he or she does get to know things. The local *recenseur* has a strange role, because she has been given the right by a distant administration to break local (and thus her own) rules of discretion: to ask direct questions and expect direct answers – to ask and to know "too much." She cannot be treated like a total stranger for she still has her place in local affairs, but she is treated with more cautiousness than she normally would be, and her

---

8 *Tu penses, ils ont la pharmacie, et il est vétérinaire. Il voit tout.*

position is certainly affected, as is always the case when an external administration imposes an office that does not fit local ways.

Otherwise, some strategic positions give people more insight than others. For example, a woman who came back to the village after more than twenty-five years away had a great deal to catch up on, as she said herself. Luckily she took care of the only gas station, and thus came to know things quickly, much faster than if she had lived on a farm. "I saw everyone go by" (*Je voyais passer tout le monde*). Observing things was not illegitimate ("too much") for her since she was a public figure running an outdoor business.

Some houses also have a better view than others. Those in the village have the best of course, because people run errands in town, and most traffic goes through that way. On the other hand, living centrally also makes one more exposed to onlookers. A woman living slightly secluded on her own private road expressed envy toward her neighbour who lived right on the public road. "You're lucky, you can see everyone passing by" (*Vous avez de la chance, vous voyez passer tout le monde*).

In general, people occupying key positions – postmen, veterinarians, doctors, mayors, *recenseurs*, shopkeepers, etc. – are thought to know more than others. As a result, they are themselves under special surveillance, not only for what they might advertently or inadvertently say, but also because their knowledge of a certain person, for instance, is expected to show in the way they react to that person, and their reactions can thus give other people clues. Of course, this is simply a refinement of the general practice of interpreting other people's social action for insight into their specific knowledge.

Staging the Exceptional

Part of anthropological and sociological theory has dealt with the ways human conduct might be analyzed as communication. Apart from studies which isolate phenomena like gestures, movements, facial expressions, etc., labelling them non-verbal communication, there have been more interesting attempts to see human conduct more as a whole, such as Goffman's studies of human interaction and the way people fashion the impressions they give others of themselves (Goffman 1959, 1974, 1981), and the classical anthropology of Victor Turner on ritual and theatre (e.g., Turner 1974, 1982).

Along with a long line of other anthropologists studying ritual, rather than isolating elements of conduct like hand gestures, these theorists have isolated *moments* of conduct, establishing a temporal instead of a spatial delimitation. Inspired by van Gennep's analysis of initiation rituals, where the initiate goes from a normal state to a liminal state and then "returns" to normal life having assumed a new role, the idea of exceptionality has prevailed in almost all performative analysis. This exceptionality or "exclusivity of states," as I would call it – also reflected in concepts like "staging," "keying," "framing," "performance" and "meta-language," to name a few performative terms – implies that one is either in one state or another, communicating on one level or another, and so on, as if life were constituted of passages between separate states and modes, with no continuity other than that of succession.

One example is Goffman's development of Bateson's discussions of play, where a specific set of conventions or a key, "transforms serious, real action into something playful" (Goffman 1959: 41-43). Meta-messages or "cues will be available for establishing when the transformation is to begin and when it is to end, namely, brackets in time" (ibid.: 45). There is "real action" as opposed to play; there is isolated, bracketed time.

If we consider all these performative concepts only as analytical tools that can order our thoughts somewhat, they might be useful; but if we use them to say something more definitive about real life, they become misleading. If things in life are considered to have continuity, it is not only because time passes by itself, and things and states are inevitably followed by others, but because part of meaning and essence remains unchanged over time, even during transformation. Otherwise, there would only be difference, only total transformation – and then "change" would have no meaning. The same goes for different communicative levels. They cannot be exclusive. Although play might be something special, it is obviously also a part of "real action."

When a mathematical curve is simplified and digitalized, the mathematician knows the exact degree of digitalization, that is, the discrepancy between the formula and the original curve. The coarser the digitalization, the less accurate is the picture of the movement produced by the formula. The mathematician also knows that the original curve is itself a mathematical product, an analogue representation of a real movement which digitalization allows us to formulate further and - re-represent. Caution should be taken, however, when human life is digitalized into time units and states, for scientists dealing with human life have no way of measuring their degree of digitalization, their discrepancy. The problem is that when one gets too far from life, the description loses likeness, validity. Instead of enlightening us, the coarseness of description blinds us.

This seems to be the case when performative terms are sought to apply to communication in La Brumaire. Either the description loses likelihood or the terms crack, first of all because, as we have seen, in La Brumaire, everything is staged. No movement, no trace is left unnoticed, by either senders or receivers. Secondly, because when engaging in one type of communication, like significant story exchange, all other types of communication are still potentially there, being evoked and giving weight to what is said or unsaid, just as talk is a part of silence and silence a part of talk. Finally, if someone blinks, it is not just a meta-message about what is being said (as "*the* message"), but meaningful communication in itself, rendering unlikely any hierarchy of expressions, meta-expressions, meta-meta-expressions and so on. For if everything by Brumairians is considered communication, it is at the same time thought to be communication about communication. Keys and frames and levels and stages interpenetrate in a communicative web so intricate that it cannot possibly be digitalized into a single, simple formula.

Furthermore, Brumairian communication also seems to disregard Turner's idea that there is on one side a rational, unvarying, "ordinary life," and on the other, a chaotic, transformative, processual, "liminality" (Turner 1986: 42). For again, since everything people do in public is read as signs by themselves and others, that is, performed with an audience in mind, it is all staged. The exceptional is part of the ordinary and vice versa, and "staging" becomes so all-encompassing that it no longer means anything – otherwise, it can only be seen as the result of anthropologists "staging" their material as they define parts of life as exceptional. When it comes to Brumairian communication, "staging" is at most a synonym for "public," implying that the private is that which is not staged, belonging to that same inviolable sphere also inhabited by "real silence." Ordinary life is certainly chaotic and processual; it is the locus of movement.

A final consequence of positing that in La Brumaire everything is communication and that, moreover, all communication is staged, and of taking Peirce's standpoint that signs need not be emitted intentionally, is the deduction that there can be no such thing as "noise." Noise is defined semiotically as anything that entails loss of information during the communication process (Greimas & Courtés 1987). Although the sound of a chainsaw may drown out human voices, making them unintelligible, it is still meaningful information in itself; both signals belong to the same communicative process of René and Jean-Pierre cutting wood together.

4.3 Conclusions on Spying

Everything that meets the eye, ear and other senses when one exposes oneself to the experiences of the landscape constitutes signs to be read and interpreted. Some of them, like gas-pipe boards and land reallotment markers, stipulate something about the local in relation to the distant, external, authoritative world. Other signs, like a passing car or a field, operate mainly within the local, as marks of action, potency, difference, and potential. All signs are the result of people moving around, living in the landscape and leaving significant traces.

Trying to establish how Brumairian sign-reading and -writing can be inserted into a broader semiotic context is partly inspired by the concept of ethnosemiotics used by Herzfeld to discuss Rhodian evil-eye accusations, Cretan sheep-stealing, and sign-systems and meaning in general, and by the fact that he leaves the concept of ethnosemiotics undeveloped with regard to semiotics in general (Herzfeld 1981b, 1983a, 1983b, 1985). Ethnosemiotics seems to refer to the idea that different "discursive spheres" represent one another. Thus, the Glendiot custom of reading the future in an animal's shoulder blade (scapulomancy) is actually more a way of probing lived social experience than talking about the future, furnishing "a diagram" or "a semiotic of prevalent social concerns," as well as being an "index" or "symbol" of political alienation from diverse forms of external officialdom (Herzfeld 1985: 247-56). Thus he uses the term "semiotic" to designate a system or domain of signs, somewhat like when I say that witchcraft and its parallel discourses may use different symbolics but they express the same social concerns, and when I talk about surfaces as systems of signs of the same type. Herzfeld would call these different semiotics.[9]

Herzfeld's opinion and mine further converge in the idea that locals – Cretans, Rhodians, Brumairians – have their own well developed and conscious systems of sign analysis (Herzfeld 1985: 46, 256), demonstrating high "semiotic sensitivity" (ibid.: 48), making the ethnographer

---

[9] Herzfeld's analysis of scapulomancy as a semiotics of prevalent concerns is analoguous to my definition of nostalgia as an interpretation of prevalent concerns in terms of evolution and "changing times": both discourses articulate temporary concerns through the dimension of time, one transposing such concerns into the future, the other into the past.

"Pignon's been working hard this winter – but he's a show-off."
"Marcel really can't fix a fence: his cows are stray again..."

just one social theoretician among many (cf. Ardener 1972b; Herzfeld 1983a).

Spying is the ongoing reading of the movements and traces of others (as well as one's own), their potency (deeds, gestures) and potential (possessions). And spying is also keeping abreast of "who is reading me."

Talking, exchanging information, is sharing and analyzing clues. Like when a police unit meets at the station to assess the current state of an investigation, the local detectives of La Brumaire meet, exchange news and evaluate the present state of village affairs using small clues to make assumptions about a broader complex of activities.

But interpreting the landscape is not mechanical, there is no dictionary translating its signs into unequivocal meaning. On the contrary, meaning is constantly being invented and invested in the signs. To talk and tell stories is to assign meaning to specific clues using all the interlocutors' common and individual experience and knowledge. This implies that, since mechanical convention does not fix the correlation between a sign and its meaning (as in language systems), it is the ever-ongoing village talk that decides how things and signs should be interpreted.

Spying adds more "fuel" to a turning mill, and talking transforms the ephemeral movements of people into temporary common knowledge. Through constant spying and talking, Brumairians engage in and develop theories of meaning, not only attaching meaning to action, but also defining and redefining meaning itself.

The limit to spying is the private. But the private is not a fixed domain, it is defined precisely by the lack of access others have to it. Like knowledge, the private is negotiable, and other people are defined by their distance from, and movement in relation to, this sphere. They can never walk into it, but they can go places that were formerly inaccessible.

There are things that should stay within the private, like odour and things that others prefer not to know. When these things escape and become public, they suddenly define others directly, by their presence, not their absence. When something becomes public, it becomes social, putting others in relation to it, like when odour put the neighbours in relationship with "evil" by cultivating their mere knowledge of it.

Nature's signs: "It's time to plant garlic."

"Might rain tomorrow..."

When there are limits to spying, it is not only because people are protecting their own private sphere against intrusion, but also because others are limiting their prying so as not to get their fingers burned.

Finally, some things spring more readily to the eye of the outsider than others; some things, signs, pass unnoticed. This is not only a question of varying knowledge and skill, but also of significance. Brumairians not only notice everything down to the smallest detail, but to them everything seems to be significant, remembered and exchanged. Nothing has "an automaton-like quality" (Ardener 1987: 49), not even a passing unknown tourist.

According to Ardener, there is a high density of significant events in remote areas (ibid.). No doubt La Brumaire can be qualified as such (see Chapter 5). Such event-density in remoteness has to do with the locals' self-defining "counter-specification" in relation to external, dominant definitions (ibid.). This is certainly the case in La Brumaire: the passing tourist is just one example, as is the infrastructural cobweb of high-tension cables, gas-pipes, highways and TGV-tracks described above. But apart from events having significance in relationship to the outside world, they mainly have significance *within*, between individuals and groups. Defining oneself against a distant and dominant outside is important, but defining oneself in relation to one's close and influential neighbours seems even more vital. The difference might be one of negotiability, that is, reciprocity: relations to the outside world seem fixed in an unbalanced situation once and for all, a perception that was only confirmed by the evolution of the land reallotment conflict. But internally, between neighbours, people can and do exert reciprocal influence, and identity is still something to be negotiated and re-formulated. Spying and talking are not just old habits from a past when they were necessary; they still seem just as vital to local social life. In fact, somehow they *are* the locus of that life.

5

The Inconsistencies of Coexistence

5.1 Being, Doing and Belonging

Let us acknowledge that stories are inquisitory tales about the doings of others; that exchange is the circulation of these stories, and of things and deeds themselves; and that spying keeps one abreast of what others are doing, and what they may know or have seen of one's own doings. This implies that social life in La Brumaire is made up of two main components, namely action, and talking about other's actions (an action in itself). Whereas action is a means of defining and redefining oneself and one's relations to others, talking is a means of defining others.

What we are dealing with is "who people are" – identity – as expressed through action, and talking about action. A person exists through his or her presence and doings, action is scrupulously followed and analyzed, and existence seems to lie in the immediate. This gives an impression of village life and identity as being rather ephemeral, non-enduring. There is action, movement and process, there is interpretation and re-interpretation, there is negotiation, definition and redefinition; rather than order, there is a striving for balance. Being is becoming, it is something ongoing.

Despite this continual "becoming," there are elements of definition that introduce something more durable. There are categories that people may belong to, and qualities that can be ascribed to them. But as we shall see, these categories and qualities are not absolute either: they are highly relative and equally negotiable, just as ephemeral as individual, social "being."

Belonging

Groups

We saw earlier how exchange- and working-groups are continuously formed, broken down and reformed, with people changing positions, allies and enemies. Such groups are formed on the basis of sympathy, common interests, political tendencies, family relations, similar ways of and attitudes towards working, and so on. When conflicts arise, be they major or minor, they immediately give rise to the formation of new and distinct groups expressing clear positions in relation to the matter and the persons involved, often cutting across and hence breaking up former groupings, and reasserting their temporality.

As we have seen, when faced with a conflict it is essential that a person choose sides, and it is even preferable that working-partners, for example, be in opposite camps than in no camp at all. Not to choose sides, not to take a position in relation to a group, even if it is only an ephemeral one, is to diminish one's social existence, and ultimately, to live in the void (*le néant*). The land reallotment conflict put two clear-cut factions into opposition – one for, the other against – but the membership of the two groups was somewhat inconstant, with people shifting from one to the other, showing allegiance to either side by engaging in exchange, talk and work with respective members and attending meetings and demonstrations or not. The President of the Association himself shifted back and forth, and even the most ardent members of the Association were not always very clear about their attitudes. They sometimes seemed quite content with the reallotment, although they always expressed varying degrees of allegiance to the opposition. Consequently, not only was membership relative, as people shifted in and out, but the actual meaning of being for or against, the content of the categories themselves, was never absolute either. People changed the content of categories through their actions. Other social groupings revolve less around conflict, but they are still ways of expressing allegiance. For example, being a blood donor seems to have much more to do with being a member of a local group, going to banquets, drinking red wine and giving blood to the same pool, than with supplying distant hospitals with the vital substance. As we saw, withdrawing from such a group can also be a strong form of expression. Ultimately, it seems that *being* a member is in itself just as important as the choice of group.[1]

This continual process of grouping and regrouping demonstrates the

---

1 And being a member of something bad is probably better than not being a member at all. Several individuals in the village are known as "*collabos*," people who collaborated with the Germans during the Occupation. The essential thing seems to be to know who they are (allegedly named on a list found by a villager), and less what they actually did. Ultimately, they just chose sides. The moniker "*collabo*" may be used to label them, but only to support a passing comment on their current behaviour. The term is never applied to denote an absolute quality in itself.

elasticity of individual membership, but more importantly, it shows the volatility of meaning itself. We might be against the reallotment, but being "against" can accommodate wide variations, including being somewhat "for." The category "against" still exists, though its content is in some way evacuated. This bears an affinity with Ardener's "hollow categories" (1972b: 69-70).

Whereas some groups of allies were formed on the basis of work, exchange and conflict, and others are continuously shifting, and thus only define and are defined by individuals for relatively short periods, certain categories of membership have something more irrevocable, almost biological, about them, and to which the label "hollow category" seems initially more difficult to apply. These categories are "family," "language" and "place:"

Family/Cousinage
In La Brumaire, everyone is related to everyone else in an extensive network that seems limitless. When a man marries, his wife's entire extended family becomes his family and vice versa, and apart from the immediate family – siblings, parents and grandparents – husband and wife no longer distinguish between cognate and affine relatives, but call everyone by the same denomination, "cousin." Furthermore, there is no distinction between first cousins and ones that are more genealogically distant. "Here, everyone is related; everyone is family" (*Ici, tout le monde est de la famille de tout le monde*), as they say. The limitlessness of the system, and the undiscriminating use of the terms "*cousin*" and "*cousine*" are very similar to Knudsen's descriptions of kinship in Corsica (Knudsen 1989a).

"Family" is thus not a very well-defined or defining category, but this does not prevent it from being used to define – quite the contrary, and perhaps precisely because it *is* so open to interpretation. Thus, a woman called a helpful relative her cousin, but when I suggested that she was also a relative of the man's brother, someone she hardly appreciated, she immediately refuted it: "Oh no, *he* is not my cousin" (*Ah non, lui, c'est pas mon cousin*). For several years, one villager was having his tractor repaired by a distant cousin, and spoke with satisfaction of their good relationship. But when the cousin charged him a rather high price for what turned out to be bad work, the first man angrily exclaimed and later often repeated: "He is no longer my cousin!" (*Il n'est plus mon cousin!*) Through the cousin's actions and the man's subsequent redefinition, a distant relationship that had been kept warm through cooperation suddenly grew cold.

The category of cousin was also skilfully negotiated in connection with the land reallotment, a conflict which often gave rise to new definitions. Persons within each camp were generally said to be linked by *cousinage* and were identified to me as cousins, whereas equally evident links between people in opposite camps were understated. An old man who was anti-reallotment, spoke of a person in the "pro" camp whom I knew to be his paternal first cousin, thus bearing the same name as himself. But instead of acknowledging him as such, the old man defined the cousin in relation to the latter's nephew by marriage – a much more distant relationship, but with someone also in the "pro" camp. The older man understated one relationship, and overstated another. In this case, camps were more defining than family, or rather, "camp" came to define "family."

As in Anne Knudsen's descriptions of the Corsican system, Brumairian kinship in itself gives no clues as to distinct family groups. Because of the possibility of choice, Corsicans, like Brumairians, emphasize some relations and under-emphasize others (cf. Knudsen 1989a). In fact, she characterizes the vendetta tradition as "the one mechanism that clearly divided kin groups and established them as discrete units" (ibid.: 311).

Unquestionably, the reallotment conflict had a similar "clarifying" effect. But that does not mean that such clarifications, which go on all the time on a smaller or larger scale, are absolutely indispensable, or that if things were not spelled out once in a while, if people didn't belong to clearly divided groups or discrete units, even ephemerally, they would not be able to orient themselves. It is one thing to describe the result of a social phenomenon, and quite another to ascribe it a social function, inferred from that result. For me, the newcomer, the reallotment process was certainly useful in getting an overview of relations and their inconstancy; and in the end, this is very probably what such clarifications constitute for everyone: social analytical tools.

That the category *cousinage* can be stretched to the extreme was further demonstrated in the case of my mother-in-law. She is of northern European origin, and was a longstanding resident of Paris, but when she moved to La Brumaire, where she had never set foot before, she was immediately supplied with a distant cousin. It turned out her late husband's grandfather was born about ten kilometres from the house she chanced to buy, and a descendant of the family was living in a hamlet nearby. For those who wished (and wish) to treat her as a local, she was simply someone who had finally come home where she belonged – *"revenue au pays."* Others could, by using different categories, still consider her a stranger.

Saying that "family" and "cousin" are hollow categories should therefore not be understood in the sense of empty or meaningless, but rather, spacious enough to contain whatever people want to, or actually do, put into them. Neither does it mean that they are of less importance than "full categories" (if such a thing even exists), for as I see it, "hollow" is not a quantitative term but a qualitative one suggesting the plastic and temporal character of categories. The way a category like "cousin" is so artistically negotiated and employed only shows how full of meaning it can be. Consanguinity does not in itself define kinship, but it still gives weight to the category.

While the horizontal aspect of kinship (that is, its spatial and synchronous dimension) seems to be negotiable, this is not so much the case with its vertical dimension, that of time and descent. The vertical reflects one's relations to specific ancestors and indicates one's place in space, in the land. Conversely, land is an image of one's position in relation to specific ancestors. To have a share in that land is to maintain one's place in the history of the family. As we saw earlier, the graveyard also merges the relations between individuals, ancestors and space in quite an explicit way.

Of course, even in its vertical dimension, kinship is not completely closed to negotiation, especially over a longer span of time, because for one thing, it is linked to possessing land, which as we have seen, has nothing enduring about it. Nevertheless, vertical kinship does seem to cling more tenaciously to individuals than relations within the horizontal dimension do (perhaps partly because when it comes to negotiating positions and relations in terms of vertical kinship, one of the protagonists – the ancestor – no longer takes active part). This ambiguity between the tenacious and negotiable features of vertical kinship reflects a more general one between the innate and achieved aspects of identity, and arises in the discussion of what I define as "qualities" further on.

Language
To some extent, people in La Brumaire speak *patois*, local dialect. Although most communication today takes place in French, almost everyone understands the *patois*. Thus speaking in dialect is not so much a question of ability, and hence restricted to certain persons or age groups, as a deliberate choice made according to circumstances. Apart from communicating information, speaking *patois* is meaningful in many other ways. This is especially true when we consider that two different *patois'*, Marchois and Berrichon, are spoken within the municipality of La Brumaire.

Distinct regional dialects like Breton, Basque, and Alsatian aside, France is linguistically divided in half by the two Romance languages, *"langue d'oïl"* in the north and *"langue d'oc"* in the south, named after the way "yes" is pronounced *"oïl"* and *"oc"* respectively (Braudel 1986: 73-78). The southern municipal border of La Brumaire coincides with county and regional borders, is also the official border between Berrichon and Marchois, and thus on a larger scale, between *langue d'oïl* and *langue d'oc*. In the Berry, people speak Berrichon and across the county border in the Marche, they speak Marchois if we are to believe the official folklorist version (e.g., de La Salle 1900, 1902; Denizet et. al. 1982).

If asked, however, villagers assert that the dividing line between Berrichon and Marchois runs right through La Brumaire and cuts the long municipality very precisely in two, more or less along a little creek, though deviating here and there to encompass one house or hamlet and exclude another. Everyone, even people who never speak *patois*, can be positioned according to this linguistic gap. "He speaks Berrichon, she speaks Marchois." So if Brumairians disagree with the official view as to where the line runs, they do agree that there is a very clear-cut line, and that it coincides with the dividing line between *"oc"* and *"oïl."* The line moves if people move, for it is they who ultimately define its course.

I have not been able to undertake a proper linguistic analysis of the two local language forms and their differences – doing so would be beyond both my scope and my competencies. Neither have I found attempts to do so by linguists or others, so instead, I have tried to establish what the differences between "*oc*" and "*oïl*" might be, and what the nature of the border that separates them is. The general impression I have obtained is that the idea of a precise dividing line is erroneous, that one should think, rather, in terms of a transitional zone several hundred kilometres wide, traversing France from east to west. As Braudel points out, "The border between the France of *oïl* and the France of *oc* is not a line that can be established once and for all" (Braudel 1986: 73).[2] L'Abbé de Sauvages continues:

> [The two regions] can only be distinguished by moving away from the belt northward or southward; then they seem to disentangle themselves little by little: for passage from one to the other is hardly abrupt; it is a question of nuances." (in Jochnowitz 1973: 27; my translation)[3]

With the exception of the words "*oc*" and "*oïl*," which according to Jochnowitz are nothing but "handy representatives," no definitive linguistic criteria have ever been established for the two languages (ibid.). It remains doubtful whether we can even conceive of them as two distinct languages, but I leave that question up to linguists.

Finally, within the two groups, and even within their sub-groups, the variations can be so wide that people of neighbouring villages cannot communicate:

> There are, both north and south of the Loire River, particular families of provincial dialects, themselves almost infinitely subdivided. ...And within these local ways of speech, from town to town, village to neighbouring village, each dialect is deformed, more or less according to the places. (Braudel 1986: 78)[4]

---

2 "...*entre la France d'oïl et la France d'oc, la frontière n'est pas une ligne repérable une fois pour toutes.*" An English edition of this work exists as *The Identity of France*, transl. by S. Reynolds, London: Collins, 1988. However, I have chosen to cite and translate excerpts from the original French edition.

3 "*On ne peut les distinguer qu'en s'écartant de la bande et allant vers le nord, ou vers le midi; ils paraissent alors se démêler peu à peu: car le passage de l'une à l'autre n'est point brusque; il se fait par des nuances.*"

4 "*Il y a, tant au Nord qu'au Sud de la Loire, des familles particulières de patois provinciaux, elles-mêmes subdivisées presque à l'infini... Et, à l'intérieur de ces parlers locaux, de bourg à bourg, de village à village voisin, chaque patois de déforme, plus ou moins selon les lieux.*"

As for the specific area under study here, Dauzat notes that

> the dialects of the Bourbonnais and the meridional Berry are still quite well preserved, but by no means homogeneous: southward, several Auvergnian and Limousine features already start appearing, with Poiterian features to the west. (Dauzat 1927: 141; my translation)5

To add to the confusion (and to justify the discretionary use of the terms, since they indeed seem to be negotiable), the geographical area "Occitanie" is defined as that part of France where *langue d'oc* is spoken, as is, more obviously, the region known as "Languedoc." The term "Languedoc" once corresponded to the medieval county of Toulouse, but today it seems to identify a much larger area coinciding with, not surprisingly, *langue d'oc* (*Larousse Illustré* 1986). Since neither Occitanie nor Languedoc are bona fide administrative units with precise borders, and since no one has actually defined *langue d'oc*, language and place categories obviously find more justification in each other than by any other criteria. All in all, what seems to underlie all this is the attempt by southern France – at different historical periods, under different reigns, representing smaller or larger fiefdoms – to oppose the political and cultural centralization of Paris, and to use language as the decisive factor.

Under these circumstances, I find it reasonable to conclude that the two different *patois* spoken in La Brumaire are both transitional forms located somewhere on a scale between "more *oc*" and "more *oïl*," rather than specimens of allegedly pure forms. That does not exclude the fact, however, that there are differences between the *patois* spoken in the north and that spoken in the south of the municipality – quite the contrary. But such differentiations should perhaps be considered along the lines of the Abbot of Sauvages's "nuances" and the deformations inherent in the infinite subdivisions of *patois* that Braudel suggests.

Whatever linguists and other scientists may say about the correctness of the content of the categories of Brumairian Berrichon and Marchois, there is no doubt that *patois* is a defining category of belonging, inclusion and sameness. It also seems to be even more definitive

---

5 "...les patois du Bourbonnais et du Berry méridonial sont encore assez bien conservés, mais n'offrent aucune homogénité: vers le sud apparaissent déjà quelques caractères auvergnats ou limousins, poiterins à l'ouest."

than the more volatile categories (e.g., family and *cousinage*) mentioned earlier. People from the south of La Brumaire who have married and moved north for example, go on being known as Marchois-speaking, although they are considered to be in solidarity with their new households. The use of these categories is strengthened by the aforementioned tendencies of people from both north and south to turn their attention in different directions, each towards their own regional centres. Conversely, turning one's back and looking the opposite way is justified by the language categories. Although it may be only about six kilometres away, some in the north call the south "the end of the earth" (*le bout du monde*), and when asked about someone from the opposite side, people tend to answer, "We don't know much about over there" (*On n'connait pas bien par là*). That may simply be the usual display of silence in response to an unwelcome question, but it is also a way of stating remoteness and opposition. At the same time it is probably true to some extent since there is less contact. Nevertheless, during the reallotment, this tendency was easily overshadowed by other, more vital concerns.

All in all, we may say the *patois* categories Berrichon and Marchois are hollow, but they are no more so than the nationally recognized categories *"langue d'oc"* and *"langue d'oïl,"* and the local categories certainly evoke the same intense north-south antagonisms. They also evoke the association of *"oc"* with Mediterranean culture, festivity, cheerfulness and generosity. As Stendahl expressed it, "It seems like joyfulness disappears with the accent" (in Braudel 1986: 77).[6] And finally, these *patois* categories seem also to share another national tendency in that their importance is stressed mainly in the south. Yet, if we asked a Toulousian, a typical *"Oc,"* he would probably consider the southern part of La Brumaire as distinctly *"oïl."*

Place
Patois may cut La Brumaire in two categorically speaking, but as with segmentary systems in general, an all-encompassing category of locality, *"chez nous"* or *"ici"* as locals would vaguely characterize it,

---

6 *"On dirait que le bonheur disparaît avec l'accent."*

overrides other, lesser divisions. *"Ici,"* "here," is a highly relative category finding its origin in each individual, for there are no natural boundaries, no encircling coasts; and there is no overall word for locals, like *"bretons"* or *"corse"* for example, with which people can all identify. The communal limits are strictly administrative, and they cut through hamlets, fields, families and ally-groups. The use of the category "Brumairians" is strictly my invention and privilege. There is no "-hood", no "-ity." Affiliation to locality is not expressed with the precision of words.

The closest one could come to an expression for the local would thus be a silent, humble and non-aggressive *"ici."* *"Ici"* is sufficiently vague, indirect, reversible, it can include (and exclude) anyone. "Here, we don't like..." (*Ici on n'aime pas...*); "Here, that's how it's done" (*Ici on fait comme ça*). And as a neighbour once said: *"Ici, on est loin de tout."* – Here, we are far from everything, here we are remote.

In fact, everything related to the outside, whether near or far, is characterized by a feeling of remoteness and insignificance, a feeling that is constantly reinforced by the presence of signs of authority in the landscape, as we have seen. The hamlet is distant from La Brumaire, where the Mayor's office and the grocers are. La Brumaire is distant from the larger neighbouring village where the bank, the pharmacy and the markets are, where services are still held in church, and where the noble, and later bourgeois landowners were established. All this is distant from the department capital, Chateauroux, and even more so from Paris, where few villagers have ever been, and even further from Brussels, where so many important decisions are taken. Exchanges with these distant, mainly administrative "outsides" are one-way, with laws, regulations, orders, taxation, agricultural restrictions and quotas coming from the outside in, and silence emanating outward from the inside.

As with *"ici,"* this "outside" is not absolute either, but defines itself to the local through a relation of inequality. Persons may belong to it if they inscribe themselves in it by their attitudes, if they "relate unequally" (cf. Herzfeld, who was kept at a polite distance because he was not able to shed the image of representing that "dominant outside" (1983a)). As with relations of inequality in general, the local reaction to the "outside" is one of silence and seclusion. In the whole process of land reallotment, which demonstrated two different and exclusive, non-communicating spheres of discourse, arose a clear example of the feeling of impotence towards a ruling "outside" – a feeling that was only confirmed in the evolution and outcome of the conflict, and which continues to be reproduced in the landscape (surfaces) and in the few direct contacts locals have with the outside. A young woman died one night in a Parisian hospital. But before her death was even officially registered, her relatives had her body smuggled out and transported home so as not to let the Parisians take possession of it. "Here, we take care of our dead ourselves" (*Ici, on s'occupe nous mêmes de nos morts*). This was not only a defensive, seclusionist act, but also an offensive utterance.

The feeling of remoteness is also indirectly evoked as something positive in the stories and knowledge people have about each other. The fact that stories suggest an awareness of actions that to outside eyes look like serious, covert and unpunished crimes, but which are mentioned locally with apparent casualness and pass without reprimand, underlines the quest for protection against outside authorities implied in remoteness. But note, such an evocation of remoteness by virtue of internal acceptance is a very powerful means of expression that bears no comparison with the above-mentioned attitude towards gossip as a functional community delimiter, pointing out insiders as well as outsiders by their ability to engage in it, expressed by Gluckman and his colleagues (cf. Chapter 2).

The vagueness and negotiability of *"ici"* has little to do with the way inhabitants of Bretagne, for example, use the word *"breton"* rather assertively to define themselves (cf. McDonald 1989). To a very high degree, language in France is a locus of identity, both in minority groups and among the French-speaking in general, and the words for various inhabitants – *"breton," "corse," "français," "alsacien"* – are also the names of their language. In La Brumaire, since there is no such distinct linguistic group, language does not supply a handy self-defining term for the local in contradistinction to a (linguistically different) "outside." The internal language categories, Berrichon and Marchois, and the category of locality expressed in *"chez nous"* and *"ici"* are not congruent.

So finally, I would argue that, unlike Corsicans and Bretons, the main and essential part of self-definition in La Brumaire takes place *within* the local, and that "place" – as well as "the local" itself for that matter

– is defined by and takes its departure from each individual, without reaching much further than the potential relations surrounding his or her respective field of tension. (This might diminish the usefulness of a distinct, common category of place that would override each individual's own social field, a fact that is further confirmed by the use of internal linguistic sub-categories.) Relations to the outside world are primarily characterized by inequality, non-exchange, non-dialogue, distance. These negative, almost non-existent relations to a dominant outside have not been provided a more self-assertive answer than the defensive, seclusionist terms *"chez nous," "ici."* The Brumairian space is a truly "remote area."

Qualities

So categories of membership, like ally-groups, family, language and place are relatively inconstant; not only do people pass in and out of them, but the categories also change meaning constantly.

Despite the impression that hardly anything is absolute in La Brumaire, certain ideas about irrevocable qualities do prevail. These are often linked to biology, to something inevitable and permanent. For example, it is assumed that personal dysfunction finds its roots in ancestral incest occurring at varying "distances" (or degrees of "closeness"). Once in a while, a certain young man succumbs to drinking and stops working. On those occasions his sister explains that their grandparents were first cousins, which is why he can't control himself and why, by the way, she herself is so ill-tempered. I had never noticed her ill-temper, but her brother's drinking obviously did make her annoyed, maybe even ill-tempered. In any case, according to a logic of reciprocal causality, what happens in the present confirms the nature of the ancestral relation, and that relation explains today's events and somehow for once puts present matters beyond the responsibility of individuals.

Typically, though, when the brother stops drinking and goes back to work, no further mention is made of the unfortunate relation between the grandparents. It can be used to explain current misfortunes, but otherwise it is not worth talking about. The cause, incest, its biological implications and its irrevocability (i.e., the whole notion of causality) vanishes along with its effects. As we saw earlier, the circumstances of one boy having a genetic deficiency and his brother being a sloppy farmer are explained by the incestuous relations of their parents, allegedly brother and sister. Their deficiency and actions only confirm the nature of the relation. But both cause and result are always mentioned together, for it is the causality that is noteworthy, not the incest itself. If there were a logic to this, it would be that people may engage in incest if they want: it is a strictly private family matter, for the results – like the incest itself – stay within the family unit, whereas the causality is universal. Somehow, the knowledge of incest is important only as a guideline to one's interaction with the affected persons and to the evaluation of their actions in the present day.

Attributing finality to genetics and biology, and making a special category of irrevocable qualities is probably invention on my part – not that I need something absolute to hold on to, but that genetics seems to me more resistant to negotiation. I don't actually think Brumairians would operate with such a hierarchy of relative absoluteness, and the way "original sin" can be used to confirm someone's present malfunction and forgotten when normalcy is resumed seems, again, to render it rather volatile.

In the same way, the orphan who inherited a farm, "building his good fortune on someone else's misfortune," seems to be criticized because he was adopted as an orphan and was not a natural son, and therefore supposedly inherited unrightfully. In fact, many people have been adopted in La Brumaire but are not exposed in the same way. Although in this case, people connect his adoptive status and his inheritance disapprovingly, the disapproval actually seems to be targeted at his behaviour in general. Of course, the fact that they use the word "orphan" and call him by his original name to discredit him plays on the idea of biological/genetic irrevocability, but the discontent is actually brought out by his present actions. Again, the categories of orphanhood and biology may make sense, but the content and the density of the categories vary constantly.

There are other irrevocable qualities that also have to do with family relations. The word *"tâche"* (stain) is used when someone does something that will have consequences for his or her family. "That's a stain on the family" (*Ah, ça tâche, ça, pour la famille*), implying that individual actions have consequences for the definition of the family.

Conversely, there are examples in stories of families with certain tendencies, like theft or arson (recall the family of fire-setters, *la famille de metteu' de feu*), that cling to the descendants. Thus, being a member of a family defines what one is liable to do, which is itself defined by what other members have done, and so on. But since family membership is relative, one can define oneself as a member (or not), for instance by doing those same things (or not). And finally, stains eventually disappear with washing, leaving traces that can only be discerned by those who want to remember. Like red wine on a white tablecloth, faulty moves and bad tendencies can be forgotten and washed away depending on one's own actions and others' interpretations – or they can be revived by repetition.

Conclusions on Being

Corsicans engage in deadly vendettas and thereby define who they are through their allegiances and enmities (Knudsen 1989a). Glendiot males from Crete engage in nightly sheep-stealing and public narratives about their sheep-stealing, thereby demonstrating that they are good at being men (or at least, good poets) and worthy allies, and thus fashioning their own identity (Herzfeld 1985). In both cases, individual action defines being – who's who, and how good they are at it. Vendettas and sheep-stealing, as demonstrative self-assertive actions, seem to be what attract the most attention, both of locals and of visiting anthropologists. As it is, the latter are more likely to have heard (and read) about these actions than to have seen them enacted. Herzfeld and Knudsen both talk about practice, but they have experienced practice represented, in texts and words (poetics, which is, of course, a practice in itself).

When it comes to La Brumaire, I too identify a great deal of self-definition in action. But what I have witnessed is both talking and action, and maybe that is why I now say that in La Brumaire, being, identity and self-definition take place somewhere between one's actions and others' talking. For identity is not something one fashions alone, there is never only *self*-definition. One furnishes signs that contribute to the ever-changing picture of who one is. Instead of just talking about oneself, one must act in order to fashion identity, and then depend on others to do the talking and finish the picture, as it looks in the present. For one's actions are not signs of oneself if there are no interpreters of those signs. Or rather, they are not social signs if there are no interpreters other than oneself.

In a social space with no borders, the "units" of belonging are constantly being defined and re-defined through action and talking about action. Every single person is at the centre of a unique system. Suspended in a network of potential relations, each person chooses to activate some of these relations and let others remain silent. Striking some chords and not others, they compose their personal "field of tension," and contribute to that of other people.

Many pages have been written about categories, identity, ethnicity, self-assertion, demonstration of group solidarity and so on. To a high degree, that is what anthropology has been about over the last few decades. Borrowing terminology and ideas from psychology, but lacking the natural limits imposed by the individual body, anthropology has been engaged in discovering how people go about inventing ways to define the invisible limits of their *social* bodies, how they "symbolize boundaries" (Cohen 1989) – from those of nations, even planets, down to the smallest entities: between and within households. Somehow, being has boiled down to this, to symbolizing boundaries – "the compelling need to declare identity is social as well as psychological" (ibid.: ix). With this "compelling need" in mind, anthropologists have set out to categorize the world and learn of other's categories, taking words like "identity" and "symbolics" so much for granted that they have received no further investigation. But do any two words really say as little as those two do? As Favret-Saada says, "all is symbolic" (personal communication), and I could add, all is identity. The interesting part is determining what things are symbolic (or signs) of, apart from the patently obvious "identity" and "boundaries," and how they acquire meaning, or more generally, how symbolizing comes about.

Over the last ten pages or so, I too have engaged in determining boundary-defining categories, but I have not done so due to any alleged "compelling need." The point for me has rather been to demonstrate the highly volatile and processual qualities of such categories, and of allegiance to them, and to show that, although people may have ordering tendencies (and I say "may," for I am not completely sure), the results of such tendencies are no more orderly than the underlying disorder. They verbalize and interpret disorder, but they do not order it.

Categories provide a point of departure for interpretation to begin, but what I analyze is not whether action fits into categories, but rather how action itself plays with, affects and changes the content of those categories and creates new meaning.

5.2 Knowledge and Meaning

In telling stories, people demonstrate their knowledge, and in keeping silent, their control of that knowledge and of the situation. Obtaining knowledge about others' doings, through spying and word-exchange, can reasonably be said to be one of the main social activities in La Brumaire, if not the primary one. Furthermore, to have knowledge is to have something to exchange – to give and withhold – and exchange is a further condition of knowing.

If one asks *why* people must know, one encounters reasoning of the order seen above – of the "compelling need" to identify, or of the individualist/materialist logic of information-management, such as "knowing even more." Otherwise, answers venture into the realms of existentialism, which though very valid, are unending and, like "compelling need," only justifiable within their own logic: to know is to participate in social life (avoiding the "*néant*"), and humans are fundamentally social. The social is also the origin of the incest prohibition, and why men exchange women: in order to be, and because they are, social and societal beings. I myself have argued that Brumairians depend on others' knowing to exist, for without others interpreting one's actions in terms of social significance, they have no such significance – an argument that falls within the same socio-existentialist logic, resting as it does on the alleged local fear of the *néant*, the social void.

Rather than focus on why, I have concentrated on asking *how*: how do people know things and, insofar as it is possible to determine, what do they know? What kind of knowledge do they attach importance to, what do they notice, into what areas of knowledge do they pry, what is relevant? The outcome of my investigation has been to characterize the circulation of knowledge as ongoing interpretation – of what people actually do, but mainly of the meaning of that doing. I have thus argued that meaning is not something inherent in things, categories and action, but that these are constantly being vested with new meaning, in relation to one another. That is why I have focused on the interplay between action and the exchange of knowledge, because that seems to be the locus of meaning-production. Meaning is neither preconceived in words nor in practice, but emerges in the interplay between the two and, therefore, between people.

I argued that this interplay and flux of meaning is in fact what telling stories and exchanging knowledge is all about: vesting behaviour and categories with their appropriate and currently agreed-upon meaning. Through this discussion, we may have also (and somehow unwillingly) come to an understanding of why talking seems to be such an important activity, and obtaining knowledge so vital, for it is actually in this continual village talking that meaning itself arises.

This takes us rather far from the idea that village talk – or gossip and rumours, as some call it – is merely functional, group-delimiting, and otherwise negative, even destructive to village life. In my opinion such talk is highly constructive, it is somehow the locus itself, the heart of village life.

Having said this, it becomes possible again to use the word "gossip," which I have otherwise so carefully avoided. When it comes right down to it, there is no doubt, of course, that this is what we are dealing with: people exchanging viewpoints about other people's movements and doings. But rather than take the negative connotations of "gossip" as a point of departure, the present study has instead argued for and, I hope, demonstrated gossip's socially constructive nature. In this sense, this work can be seen to rehabilitate gossip, placing it alongside all the noble societal phenomena that are normally considered the proper objects of anthropological investigation.

Seeing village talk as the negotiation of meaning also demonstrates the limitations of concepts like "social order" and "norms," usually used in discussions of individual conduct and collective reflections on that conduct, for these concepts appear unable to accommodate the dynamics of village life and of meaning. Stories do not stipulate norms, they investigate actions and re-actions; and actions are not performed according to the "norms" of what is acceptable, but rather the acceptable, the socially possible, is continuously being invented and reinvented through peoples' doings and others' interpretations of those doings.

As I said elsewhere, instead of considering village talk as establishing a social order, it would be more appropriate to perceive talk as a kind of social cartography bearing closer resemblance to daily, shifting weather reports than to geographical maps. And instead of seeing talk as enforcing local norms, it seems to make more sense to conceive what we could call a *"champ du possible,"* a field of what is possible, defined through actions and reactions, talking among them. For if we take into account that what many people are supposed to have done falls far beyond what is normally and officially considered acceptable behaviour, it becomes difficult to maintain that actions are governed by norms, and that deviation from norms is condemned. Village talk does not condemn action according to a set of preconceived norms, it finds meaning in that action, and understanding of its social consequences – what others can get away with. And that seems to be quite a lot.

Ultimately, the consequence of approaching social life this way is that the individual is shifted into the centre, not only of the analysis, but of social life itself; and the image of village morality as something terribly harsh and difficult to live, driven by abstract "collective needs," is modified, changed into something moving, active, "unofficial" and permissive, and something the individual has direct influence upon: not repressive, but revelatory.

A final question regarding norms: can a semiotic approach be maintained that holds up to the following definition of Eco?: "The task of semiotics is to isolate different systems of signification, each of them ruled by specific norms, and to demonstrate that there is signification and that there are norms" (Eco 1973: 60).

Norms are apparently what link signs to their meanings. If that is so, when people concur that the sound of Jean-Pierre's chainsaw emanating from René's farm is a sign of their renewed relation, the signification would be the renewed relation, and the norm, that when people are on good terms, they lend each other chainsaws. In that sense, norms are not so much features that guide people's actions as analytical tools to understand those actions, and furthermore, norms are statistical averages, continually deduced from action, just as meaning is. They are not imposed "from above" (or "below"), they are created and revised through action and analysis. As shown in Chapter 4, talking implies agreeing upon the present conventions linking sign to meaning. For the time being, it seems that when people are on good terms they tend to lend each other equipment, and conversely, when people want to show they are on good terms, they can do it by lending each other equipment.

Finally, a word about resonance. "*Ça résonne*," a villager said of an old surname still applied to descendants of the person originally named with it. "*Ça résonne, ce nom là*" (That name strikes a chord; it resonates), because the name both adds historical weight to the social being of the descendant, and at the same time acquires new content through his doings. Wikan uses "resonance" to describe the mutual understanding that can arise between people of very different cultures (Wikan 1992), but I find the notion equally evocative when used temporally to apply to meaning, describing the phenomenon where stories and ideas travel through time and space and are kept alive, like a surname. The echo goes on emanating meaning, but the originating sound and its sense are transformed by the contours of what they encountered along the way. At the same time, the echo recounts its journey: as in the sonar system of a bat, the echo conveys a vague image of the contours it met, tracing the objects and walls that, when struck, did not absorb it, but re-articulated it, deflected it, sending it further.

Used in the temporal sense, the notion of resonance could also be applied to myths, and to so-called oral traditions in general. For if certain stories, myths, poems and songs go on being told, sung and recited, it is because they go on making sense, in the triple meaning of the expression (producing sense, conveying sense, making people sense), whereas those forgotten have lost their relevance: they have stopped being resonant because they no longer contribute meaning to, or are supplied with new energy from, that which they encounter.[7] In that way, a cultural phenomenon not only says something about a "today" where it can be experienced and a past where it arose, but also about the whole period in between when it went on "making sense."

---

7 The notion of resonance can thus be assimilated to what Sperber calls cognitive interpretation and mnemotic selection in relation to the transformations of myths (cf. my Chapter 2.4: Sperber 1972: 115).

5.3 Paradoxes of Coexistence

Looked upon superficially and from the outside, life in La Brumaire seems quite stable and unchanging: people going to their fields, tending their animals, helping each other with daily chores, attending the occasional christening or funeral (the latter more often than the former). Days and weeks go by, nothing changes except the weather, then the seasons, each one bringing with it other tasks: ploughing, sowing, assisting calving, harvesting, and eventually, ploughing again. *Toujours la même chose.*

But upon closer examination, the picture changes; as a result of replacing institutions and roles with acting individuals, and attributing each of them with significance as I have tried to do here, Brumairian life becomes terribly transitory and intangible, made up of action, movement, choice, formation and disintegration, and ephemeral meaning continually reinterpreted. Nothing seems formalized; no norms set the limits.

And yet again, with time, something else emerges as more durable, and more enduring, than the ongoing fluctuations of daily life. That "something" keeps recurring, articulated in life by almost everything people do and say, and seemingly paradoxical. We have already detected the paradox in various relationships: in dialogue, between silence and constant talking; in exchange, between giving and withholding; in stories, between simultaneous condemnation and acceptance; and in Jeanne's curtains, that osmotic membrane between "inside" and "outside."

What is reflected in these relations, and in other similar ones, is an overall paradox between dependency and autonomy that is itself a reflection of the mutual control and influence that villagers have and exert upon each other's lives. I call this paradoxical, because one of the qualities of paradox is that by definition it contains no possible mediation; it cannot be overcome. There is no right distance between people, no perfect flow of information – "just enough" does not exist. Jeanne will never get those perfect curtains that let just the right amount of information slip between inside and outside: such curtains do not exist.

Cohen has investigated how individuality and collectivity could be expressed simultaneously without compromising each other, and found the answer in symbolism and statements of identity (Cohen 1986: ix).

I argue that there is no answer: individuality and collectivity do compromise each other and *that* is the dynamic between them. Gullestad has investigated how Norwegian urbanites, "facing acute tensions between individuality and sociability...use different kinds of symbolic means to establish social boundaries...symbolic 'fences'" (Gullestad 1986: 52). But in meshing output and program, syntagmatic and paradigmatic statements (cf. Ardener 1971b: 55) like Cohen does, and with a somewhat utilitarian view of symbolism, Gullestad apparently thinks that definitive distances can be established between individuality and sociability, and that a perfect fence exists which can dissolve or mediate the tension. Finally, she sees this tension – and I have also been pointing in a similar direction – as a part of the human condition. But again, where she thinks this tension can be overcome, I do not.

I have argued that although individuals are continually challenging each other, their ultimate need is social. They exist as individuals by virtue of their difference from other individuals, and they exist as social beings by their likeness to others. Somehow I believe that the idea of an "original collectivity" is just as historically conditioned as any other (cf. Rorty 1989: 189-90), and my belief is only confirmed by Brumairians, whose notion of being someone within an "us" is matched by their fear of other members of that "us," precisely because they are all members and all close to one another. There is mutual control and influence: that is both good and bad, and must be negotiated in the best way. But negotiation never leads to a mediation, a solution to the conflict, a dissolution of the paradox.

Let us return to village life, for here the idea of paradox is coupled with and articulated in praxis through the notion of balance. But just as paradox cannot be mediated, balance cannot be achieved, only striven for. There is never the right amount, always both too much and not enough. When cautiously approaching everything they and others do, Brumairians are "balancing" – in drinking, blood-sausage-giving, practising witchcraft, exchanging words, working, and in exchange in general. But note that though balance is expressed in exchange, it is never established, and that we are talking about balance between individuals, not in society in general. People may strive for balance, societies do not.

Balance has to do with potency and potential, but that it cannot be final is confirmed again by the fact that no one really knows the potential of another since wealth is kept secret. If people spoke openly of their wealth, they might be positioned accordingly, and that would most probably violate the foundations of balance and equality. Balance therefore has to do with ongoing exchanges and not so much with the actual potential that lies behind them. According to Piot, secrecy is also linked to a principle of interpersonal balance among the Kabre of northern Togo. But there, "lack of hierarchy – equality – is ambiguous and undesirable" (Piot 1993: 362). In La Brumaire, the situation is the opposite; but finally, hierarchy and equality are two sides of the same thing, namely balance. The essential thing is that people are putting commodities – things, deeds, words – on a scale and negotiating paradox.

It turns out that I have been inescapably drawn to finding something enduring in the untidiness of daily life in La Brumaire. What I ended up with has an almost inherent justification: that humans are profoundly both social and individual, and that the tension between these two "natural" tendencies gives rise to a series of smaller paradoxes all reflecting a larger one, namely the balance between autonomy and dependency.

It is not my impression, though, that Brumairians would consider themselves governed by such natural and enduring tendencies. They find that times are changing, that things don't endure, and regret that people are increasingly occupied with themselves and less with others – more autonomous and less dependent. This does not mitigate the overarching principle of balance between the two, however, and I attribute Brumairian reasoning to using time and the past to express something about tensions that actually exist in the present. Nostalgia never deals exclusively with the past, it is mainly a comment upon the present. By using the word "enduring," I suggest simultaneity – that the same principle of balance recurs in different spheres – rather than historical durability. In that sense, the Brumairian analysis is right, things do change, as do principles. Richard Rorty suggests that even the idea (in this case, my idea) of the natural solidarity of humankind is an historical contingency (Rorty 1989), and thus is evanescent.[8] If he's right, I'll get over it with time – it seems.

---

[8] Rorty does not dismiss solidarity. On the contrary, he advocates solidarity that goes beyond present ethnocentric tendencies, that is based on the will to recognize the sufferings of others, and not on a supposedly inherent human solidarity.

5.4 On Anthropologizing

What, actually, is the difference between what Brumairians might say about their lives (or could say, since they do not say much about themselves) and what I, the anthropologist, may say?

I have claimed that to a large extent, I was learning from them, not only about their social knowledge, but also about how to obtain and analyze that knowledge. Like me, they are interested in knowledge, and in knowledge about knowledge; not only do they move around on some primary level, from which I, the scholar, then deduce other, more intricate levels of knowledge; they too use ladders. But it is hard to believe there is no difference other than the fact that I will write something afterwards. It is clear to me that the old notions of objectification do not in themselves establish a difference between us: I was just as much an object as they were. And I know that if they had not accepted and sometimes even enjoyed my presence, I would have remained the sole and only object. They let me objectify them and vice versa, because under the circumstances it was necessary and desirable, and because objectifying is one of their ways as well.

The differences between anthropologists and their objects are usually posited in terms of power. The normal situation, and a general criticism of anthropologists, is that they usually study people who are somehow "inferior to," "less powerful" than themselves, and that they profit from the unequal distribution of roles and the one-way flow and consumption of items and information that characterize both colonialism and neo-colonialism (cf. Stocking 1983). Staying within Europe does not change the picture. As Anne Knudsen says, anthropologists seldom study people who are richer or more powerful than themselves for the simple reason that being studied can be unpleasant, and only the high and mighty have the power to prevent one from objectifying them (Munk 1991).

But in La Brumaire, studying and being studied are part of being alive and social; these activities belong to and are conceivable within the local sphere of action. Writing down what one has learned is of course something else, but does not in itself define a difference of analysis as far as I can see, although the analysis develops in the process of writing. One could argue that I am literary, they are not, but that does not in itself account for a difference. Literacy is often coupled with power, but in this case, I hardly think my academic background made my analysis more refined than theirs.

Obviously, I am trying to steer clear of simple *a priori* tendencies and dismiss the idea that pre-established categories – e.g. "us" and "them," scholars and their objects, writers and non-writers, or passersby and residents – might account for eventual differences in levels of analysis. I have argued that no one in La Brumaire was strictly definable, but that all being was continuously in the process of becoming. Of course, that is my point of view, my interpretation of local ways; but if this also seems probable to the locals, then there would be no definite and ultimate category defining a difference between "them" and me – for who are "they," other than an undefined number of heterogeneous people, associating and dissociating in gatherings which (as they did for everyone) sometimes included me and sometimes did not? Universally, the situation is one of "I" and "others," not "us" and "them."

If categories cannot account for a difference between the locals' analysis versus that of a passing anthropologist, what else might? Let us look at the object of it all, talking, silence and knowledge:

1) I talk about them, they do not talk about themselves, but neither do I talk about myself. They talk about others, which is also what I am doing.

2) They talk about what others do, but in the sense of: what does the subject's behaviour mean (and what does it do to meaning itself)? They look for underlying meaning just like I do. The question is, how far do each of us go? I ended up finding fundamental paradoxes that deal with coexistence and the balance between dependency and autonomy, but I was not specifically looking for them when I set out, they basically leapt out at me (or rather, we invented them together). These paradoxes were evoked or expressed in a more-or-less condensed form in much of what my interlocutors did and said. Someone else might have found something different, but I found those, and I did not find them alone. Meaning cannot be found alone in La Brumaire.

A gold-digger enters someone else's land and starts washing gold in the river. Eventually, she concentrates tiny grains of gold dust in her pan; there they lie, sparkling; she will melt them into a little, solid lump. Market conventions aside, who would be the richest: the gold-digger, who concentrated an immensely small part of what is really there, or the landowner, who possesses all that gold in dispersed and diluted form? My point is that richness prevails, whether more or less diluted. The question remains, do Brumairians only own their knowledge in diluted form? Is my lump of gold that different? I do not know.

3) One thing is certain, though: whereas gold still has value off the land, knowledge, like in sorcery, only has value on the terrain where it originates, in the immediate. Brumairians talk to each other, whereas I suppose that, in the end, I am talking mainly to fellow researchers. When it comes to the receivers of the analysis, mine and theirs, there is a categorical difference. I am addressing someone who is definitely outside the talked-about persons' social field, which, as we saw, makes no sense in La Brumaire: I am talking just for the sake of talking (which in academia constitutes making a career), not because the listener needs that knowledge to act (cf. Favret-Saada 1977).[9] Therein lies a difference: I wouldn't learn to be discreet enough, to mind my tongue; I just had to go around squawking to others. That still does not account for a difference of analysis though.

Maybe I should give up altogether the dualistic idea of differentiating between "their" version and "my" version: such a dichotomy even seems to run contrary to everything else I have said. Perhaps my analysis is like anyone's in ways I have already demonstrated – yet at the same time, it is different, because I am a different person with a different history, operating from within my specific "field of tension." But that holds true for all of us: me, any Brumairian, anyone else delving into the knowledge of that place at that time. As we have seen, the ethnologist's analysis of a myth is just another variation of it (Lévi-Strauss

---

9   As Favret-Saada says, there is always a reason to talk in sorcery (1977), yet she does not reflect on the fact that her *readers* get to know things just for the sake of knowing. Then again, she is convinced that her knowledge could have a therapeutic effect, not on the vital force of any given household in this case, but on an academic discipline that needs to be cured of dealing with sorcery on a very superficial level without listening to or taking part in crises of sorcery themselves. "I was struck by the fact that the impact of my work on the specialized literature was almost nothing" (*J'ai été frappée de ce que l'impact de mon travail ait été à peu près nul sur la litterature spécialisée*) (Favret-Saada 1987: 19; my translation).

& Eribon 1988: 196). Of course, this is not completely satisfactory reasoning, especially since Lévi-Strauss was never able to show us the relationships between different versions and the mechanisms that transform one into another. He had to be content with suggesting that one myth gives meaning by reference to another myth, which itself refers to another, and so on, in the same way that words in a dictionary can only be defined by each other (ibid.: 198). How my version is related to any local version cannot be accounted for by Lévi-Strauss's analysis of myth transformations. His analysis can only establish that these versions are related, and that they say the same things in different ways.

Finally, what I say about life in La Brumaire is probably not fundamentally different from what any Brumairian would say; there is no big (categorical) difference. I have not discovered the paradigms of their daily syntagmatic doings and words; those paradigms are there, albeit in a different form, in that daily stream of events (Ardener 1978), and people do recognize them. I probably crystallize them a little more, and I write them down which gives them another status. I do not raise Brumairian paradigms as timeless, placeless truths though, but keep them at the level of historical probability (cf. Hastrup 1986).

My purpose for knowing and talking is not the same as a local's. Although, like I do, a local person collects and collages (*bricole*) bits and pieces from here and there to make a finished, if changeable picture, that picture has implications for his or her subsequent doings and talkings, determining which baker to buy bread from, whether or not to go to the blood-donor banquet this year, how much to tell to the next-door neighbour, what to think about so-and-so's illness, and so on; whereas for me, who no longer take part in that life on a daily basis, the picture will serve as important knowledge if and when I go on to other fields, when I read other theories of coexistence in Europe and elsewhere (offices, space-shuttles, oil-rigs, etc.) or when I hear about others' field experiences. For although what I have described here is not universal, it is certainly not exclusively Brumairian either.

What, indeed, is left for me but to hope that others who do read me and *hear*, without having a reason for knowing, will take some pleasure in doing so and might, if they didn't already, come to acknowledge life and coexistence in one little French village in the 1990's as something more alive, creative and non-stigmatizing than they had previously assumed. That would be my best reason for getting my hands dirty, and for telling.

Reflections upon a Moving Field

Throughout this text I have reflected on the way I inserted myself in the local social surroundings, how my position was evaluated and negotiated by my interlocutors and myself, and what the conditions for my access to knowledge, and thus meaning, were. When I take a final reflective stance, the object of reflection is no longer my involvement while in the field, but now that I am home, how my work inscribes itself in another transient field, that of the discipline of anthropology, and how that discipline has also conditioned my approach to knowledge and meaning. Although I feel I spent three or four years in isolation, with little academic contact, what I have written clearly does not take its own tangent, but follows a series of other related works. This leads me to acknowledge that, although one might feel isolated from spheres of intellectual influence, one never is. Ideas are conceived and circulate just as much "out there" in daily life as in ethnographic colloquia.

Seen in the general context of a discipline, the following tendencies can be noted:

1) The shifting of the individual into the centre, thus giving room to the variety of individual interpretations.

2) The idea that the individual should not necessarily be seen in opposition to a social or collective.

3) The very basic idea that everyday life is just as evocative and full of meaning as more ritualized life, and in this specific case, that the ritual, the exceptional, is an integral part of ordinary life, and that everything is exceptional.

4) Perhaps most importantly, the idea that meaning is created and re-created, not preconceived; it is mediated through the actions, reactions and re-actions of individuals rather than governed by overall systems and norms. This idea could be characterized as a pragmatic approach to culture, and to life in general. Such a view is becoming more and more common, making me think that social scientists have been able to

overcome the obstacle of dealing with practice without being materialistic, dealing with individuals without being utilitarian, and dealing with meaning without being linguistically deterministic.

Just as life in La Brumaire is not made up of discrete stages, our discipline does not advance by jumping from one exclusive sphere of thinking to the next (cf. Renato Rosaldo's critique of Kuhnian paradigms (1989: 231, n. 14)). The past still endures in the present. Even if functionalism, for example, has been dismissed in its pure form, functionalist ideas still contribute to anthropological analysis alongside other forms and elements of reasoning. As well, what we invent today will not disappear, but will contribute to the further development of ideas.

The current trend seems to be to ask how rather than why, which gives quite different results. The present work has wrestled constantly with how and why, "how" desperately struggling for ascendancy. Simply asking "Why?" often takes the object of the matter as a given parameter or precept – as in "Why do people gossip?" – and proceeds to seek answers beyond the object itself. "How?" sets out to investigate that very object, the talking itself, only to discover that it was not at all what it was thought to be.

BIBLIOGRAPHY

Abrahams, R.D.
   1970 "A performance-centred approach to gossip," *MAN*, vol. 5, pp. 290-301.

Alphandéry, P., P.Bitoun & Y. Dupont
   1988 *Les champs du départ – une France rurale sans paysans ?*, Paris: Editions la Découverte.

Ardener, E.
   1970 "Witchcraft, economics, and the continuity of belief," in: M. Douglas, ed.: *Witchcraft confessions and accusations*, London: Tavistock, pp. 141-60.
   1971a "Social anthropology and language," in: Ardener 1989, pp. 1-44.
   1971b "The new anthropology and its critics," in: Ardener 1989, pp. 45-64.
   1972b "Language, ethnicity and population," in: Ardener 1989, pp. 65-71.
   1978 "Some outstanding problems in the analysis of events," in: Ardener 1989, pp. 86-104.
   1987 "'Remote areas': some theoretical considerations," in: A. Jackson, ed.: *Anthropology at Home* (ASA Monograph no. 25), London: Tavistock, pp. 38-54.
   1989 *The Voice of Prophecy and Other Essays*, M. Chapman, ed., Oxford: Basil Blackwell.

Barthes, R.
   1973 *Mythologies*, London: Paladin Books.
   1985 *L'aventure sémiologique*, Paris: Editions du Seuil.

Bergmann, J.R.
   1987 *Klatsch – Zur sozailform der diskreten indiskretion*, Berlin/N.Y.: Walter de Gruyter.

Bernard, D.
   1982 *Paysans du Berry dans la France ancienne: la vie des campagnes berrichonnes*, Roanne: Horvath.

Boncoeur, J.-L.
   1983 *Le diable aux champs*, Paris: Fayard.

Bourdieu, P.
   1977 "Le pouvoir symbolique," *Annales*, vol. 32, no. 3.

Braudel, F.
   1986 *L'identité de la France I – Espace et histoire*, Paris: Editions Arthaud.

Certeau, M. de
  1990 *L'invention du quotidien 1 – arts de faire*, Paris: Editions Gallimard.
Clifford, J. & G.E. Marcus
  1986 *Writing Culture: the Politics and Poetics of Ethnography*, eds., Berkeley: University of California Press.
Cohen, A.
  1986 *Symbolising Boundaries: Identity and Diversity in British Cultures*, ed., Manchester University Press.

Dauzat, A.
  1927 *Les patois – évolution, classification, étude*, Paris: Delagrave.
Denizet, J. et. al.
  1982 *Berry*, Le Puy-en-Velay: C. Bonneton.

Eco, U.
  1973 "Social life as a sign system," in: D. Robey, ed.: *Structuralism: An Introduction*, Oxford: Clarendon Press, pp. 57-72.
  1976 *A Theory of Semiotics*, Indiana University Press.
Eliade, M.
  1963 *Aspects du mythe*, Paris: Editions Gallimard.

Favret-Saada, J.
  1971 "Sorcières et lumières," *Critique*, no. 287, april 1971.
  1977 *Les mots, la mort, les sorts*, Paris: Editions Gallimard.
  1980 *Deadly Words – Witchcraft in the Bocage*, transl. by C. Cullen, Cambridge: Cambridge University Press. (English edition of Favret-Saada 1977).
  1986 "L'invention d'une théraphie: la sorcellerie bocaine, 1887-1970," *Le Débat*, mai-september, no. 40.
  1987 "Les culottes Petit-Bateau: dix ans d'études sur la sorcellerie en France," *Gradhiva*, no. 3.
  1989 "Unbewitching as therapy," *American Ethnologist*, pp. 40-56.
Favret-Saada, J. & J. Contreras
  1981 *Corps pour corps – Enquête sur la sorcellerie dans le Bocage*, Paris: Editions Gallimard.

Gluckman, M.
  1963 "Gossip and scandal," *Current Anthropology*, vol. 4, pp. 307-15.
  1968 "Psychological, sociological and anthropological explanations of witchcraft and gossip: a clarification," *MAN*, vol. 3, pp. 20-34.

Goffman, E.
  1959 *The Presentation of Self in Everyday Life*, New York: Doubleday.
  1974 "Keys and keyings," in: *Frame Analysis*, New York, pp. 40-82.
  1981 *Forms of Talk*, Oxford.
Greimas, A.J. & J. Courtés
  1987 *Semiotik – sprogteoretisk ordbog*, Århus: Basilisk.
Gullestad, M.
  1986 "Symbolic 'fences' in urban norwegian neighbourhoods," *Ethnos*, vol. 51, no. 1-2, pp. 52-70.

Handelman, D.
  1973 "Gossip in encounters: the transmission of information in a bounded social setting," *MAN*, vol. 8, no. 2, pp. 210-27.
Hastrup, K.
  1986 "Sandhed og synlighed – autenticitetsproblemet i antropologien," Nordisk Etnografmøde, Stockholm, (publ. in english in: *Folk*, vol. 28).
  1992 *Det antropologiske projekt – om forbløffelse*, København: Nordisk.
Herzfeld, M.
  1981b "Meaning and morality: a semiotic approach to evil eye accusations in a greek village," *American Ethnologist*, vol. 8, pp. 560-74.
  1983a "Looking both ways: the ethnographer in the text," *Semiotica*, vol. 46, Amsterdam: Mouton Publishers, pp. 151-166.
  1983b "Signs in the field: prospects and issues for semiotic ethnography," *Semiotica*, vol. 46, no. 2-4, Amsterdam: Mouton Publishers, pp. 99-106.
  1985 *The Poetics of Manhood – Contest and Identity in a Cretan Mountain Village*, Princeton: Princeton University Press.
Holmberg, D.H.
  1989 *Order in Paradox – Myth, Ritual, and Exchange among Nepal's Tamang*, Ithaca/London: Cornell University Press.

Jochnowitz, G.
  1973 *Dialect Boundaries and the Question of Franco-Provençal*, Paris/The Hague: Mouton.

Kapferer, B.
  1975 "Anthropology and gossip – Correspondence," *MAN*, vol. 10, pp. 617-18.
Kapferer, J.-N.
  1990 *Rumeurs – le plus vieux média du monde*, Paris: Editions du Seuil.

Knudsen, A.
1989a *En ø i historien: Korsika – historisk antropologi 1730-1914*, København: Basilisk.
1989b "Tavshed er magtens tegn – prestige, ære og magt i de mediterrane samfund," in: L.W. Pape et al., eds.: *Magt – kultur, livsformer og køn*, Århus: Årbog for kvindeforskning.

La Salle, L. de
1900 *Souvenirs du vieux temps*, Paris: Maisonneuve & Larose, (estimated date).
1902 *Moeurs et coutumes*, Paris: Maisonneuve & Larose, (estimated date).
Lancaster, W.
1974 "Anthropology and gossip – Correspondence," *MAN*, vol. 9, pp. 626-27.
Lévi-Strauss, C.
1955 "The structural study of myth," in: T.A. Sebeok, ed.: *Myth – A Symposium*, Indiana University Press, 1972.
1979 *La voie des masques*, Paris: Librairie Plon.
Lévi-Strauss, C. & D. Eribon
1988 *De près et de loin*, Paris: Editions Odile Jacob.

Mauss, M.
1954 *The Gift – Forms and Functions of Exchange in Archaic Societies*, London: Routledge & Kegan Paul, 1970.
McDonald, M.
1989 *'We are not French!' – Language, Culture and Identity in Brittany*, London: Routledge & Kegan Paul.
Morin, E.
1969 *La rumeur d'Orleans*, Paris: Editions du Seuil.
Muchembled, R.
1991 *La sorcière au village (XVe-XVIIIe siècle)*, Paris: Editions Gallimard.
Munk, M.
1991 "På ekspedition i overklassen," *Weekendavisen* ,1/2-1991, p. 18.

Ongka
1979 *Ongka – A Self-Account by a New Guinea Big-Man*, transl. by A. Strathern, London: Duckworth.

Paine, R.
  1967 "What is gossip about? An alternative hypothesis," *MAN*, vol. 2, pp. 278-85.
  1968 "Gossip and transaction," *MAN*, vol. 3, pp. 305-9.
Piot, C.D.
  1993 "Secrecy, ambiguity, and the everyday in Kabre culture," *American Anthropologist*, vol. 95, no. 2, pp. 353-370.

Rochet-Lucas, B.
  1980 *Rites et traditions populaires en Bas-Berry – pélérinages et diableries*, Chateauroux: Imprimerie Badel.
Rorty, R.
  1989 *Contingency, Irony, and Solidarity*, Cambridge: Cambridge University Press.

Segalen, M. & F. Zonabend
  1987 "Social anthropology and the ethnology of France: the field of kinship and the family," in: A. Jackson, ed.: *Anthropology at Home* (ASA Monograph no. 25), London: Tavistock, pp. 110-19.
Sperber, D.
  1973 *Le structuralism en anthropologie*, Paris: Editions du Seuil.
Stocking Jr., G.W.
  1983 *Observers Observed: Essays on Ethnographic Fieldwork*, ed., Madison: University of Wisconsin Press.

Turner, V.
  1974 *Dramas, Fields and Metaphors: Symbolic Action in Human Society*, London: Cornell University Press.
  1982 *From Ritual to Theatre*, New York: Performing Arts Journal Press.
  1986 "Dewey, Dilthey, and drama: an essay in the anthropology of experience," in: Turner & Bruner 1986, pp. 33-44.
Turner, V. & E. Bruner
  1986 *The Anthropology of Experience*, eds., Illinois University Press.

Wikan, U.
  1992 "Beyond the words: the power of resonance," *American Ethnologist*, vol. 19, no. 3, pp. 460-82.

INDEX

A
Abrahams, R.D. 34
actions (see also 'being defined through action,' 'discourse and action' 'doings') 69, 135, 175, 188-190, 191-193, 202
– and meaning 190, 191-193, 202
– as signs 25, 135
Alphandéry, E., B. Bitoun & Y. Dupont 13
Ardener, E. 18, 26, 66, 104-106, 109, 112, 129, 144, 158, 169, 171, 177, 196, 201
Augé, M. 74

B
Barthes, R. 65, 137, 141, 149, 158
Bateson, G. 164
bavard(e) 78, 117
being (see also 'identity, being and becoming') 10, 24, 175-177, 188-190
– defined through action 188
belonging (see also 'identity') 25, 33, 175-186, 189
– and family 177-180, 187-188
– and groups 175-177
– and *ici* 183-186
– and language (see also '*berrichon*,' '*marchois*,' '*patois*') 180-183, 185
– and place 183-186
Bergmann, J.R. 34,
Bernard, D. 22, 42, 57
berrichon 23, 180, 182-183, 185
bien causer 78
blood 39-40, 54, 109

Boncoeur, J.-L. 22, 98, 99
Bourdieu, P. 156
Braudel, F. 180, 181, 182, 183

C
causality 113-114, 186
Certeau, M. de 135, 153-154, 158
Clifford, J. & G.E. Marcus 119
Cohen, A. 189, 195-196
communication (see also 'exchange of words,' 'talking') 9-10, 73-75, 163-166
– and staging 163-166

D
Dauzat, A. 182
Denizet, J. 22-23, 180
discretion 9, 46, 63, 73-75, 80, 83-84
– indirect speech 80-83
– principles of 80-88
discourse (see also 'witchcraft and parallel discourse,' 'witchcraft and rational discourse') 24-27, 92-95, 97, 100-107, 128
– and actions 25
– and external categories 26-7
– and inconstancy 27
doings (see also 'actions') 10

E
Eco, U. 137-139, 193
Eliade, M. 65
ethnosemiotics 25, 167
exchange 9, 21-22, 27, 32, 47, 59-62, 69, 104, 107, 119, 121-122, 126-131, 169, 175, 191, 195-197

– and reciprocity 110-112, 114, 118, 129-131
– and tug-of-war games 115-119, 127
– and withholding 119
– balance of 21, 59-60, 112-115, 196-197
– of deeds 108-112, 129-131
– of goods 108-112, 129-131
– of words (see also 'communication,' 'talking') 73-74, 84-85, 116-119, 126-131
– principles of 112-119, 129-131
– the paradox of 195-197
everyday life 202

F

Favret-Saada, J. 24, 26, 55, 92-98, 100, 103-106, 113-114, 121, 122, 123, 126, 128, 162, 189, 200
Favret-Saada, J. & J. Contreras 24
field of tension 47, 107, 189
fieldwork 9, 10, 119-121
– anthropologist's position 12-17, 26, 84-85, 96-98, 119-128
– anthropologist as *prise* 97, 122-128
flatteur/flatteuse 79, 161

G

Gennep, A. van 164
gift-giving (see also 'exchange') 108, 113-114, 118
Gluckman, M. 33-34, 185
Goffman, E. 163-164
gossip 32-34, 192
Greimas, A.J. & J. Courtes 166
Gullestad, M. 196

H

Handelman, D. 34
Hastrup, K. 35, 119, 201
Herzfeld, M. 12, 17, 24-25, 26, 128, 167, 169, 184, 188
hollow categories 177, 179

I

identity (see also 'being,' 'belonging,' 'signs and identity') 10, 24-25, 45, 171, 175, 188-190, 195
– being and becoming 175
irrevocable qualities 186-188

J

Jochnowitz, G. 181

K

Kapferer, B. 34
Kapferer, J.-N. 34, 61
kinship, (see also 'belonging and family') 177-180
Klatsch 34
knowledge 9-11, 26, 36, 47, 49-51, 69, 73-75, 107-108, 191-192, 198-202
– and anthropologizing 198-203
– and children's talk 57
– and ongoing interpretation 191
Knudsen, A. 25-26, 115, 118, 120, 177, 178, 188, 198

L

La Brumaire 9, 18-23
– demographic situation 20
– economy and wealth 20-22, 108-112, 114-115
La Salle, L. de 22, 82, 180
Lancaster, W. 34

INDEX

land reallotment 12-17, 56, 58, 87-88, 120-122, 154, 176, 178
landscape 135, 144, 151-160, 169
– and itinerary 154
– and maps 154-156
– and traces 135
– as signs (se also 'signs, surfaces as') 158, 169
– as text 135
Le Berry 22-23
Lévi-Strauss, C. 65-66, 109, 129, 200-201
Lévi-Strauss, C. & D. Eribon 65-66, 200-201
lying 86-88

M

Malinowski, B. 106
Mauss, M. 108, 113, 118, 129-130
marchois 23, 180, 182-183, 185
McDonald, M. 185
meaning (see also 'actions and meaning,' 'signs, interpretations of,' 'signs and meaning,' 'silence and meaning') 9-10, 25-26, 135-143, 169, 191-194, 202-203
– and resonance 194
– and the interpreting individual 26
– the volatility of 177
Morin, E. 34
Muchembled, R. 105
Munk, M. 198
myth (see also 'stories and myths') 65-68, 200-201
mythicality defined 68

N

nostalgia 130, 197
norms 192-193, 195

O

odour 36-38, 49-50, 65-66
objectification 198
Ongka 113

P

Paine, R. 34
paradoxes (see also 'silence and speech, the paradox of,' 'exchange, the paradox of,' 'stories, the paradoxes of') 11, 46, 195-197, 199
– and the notion of balance 196-197
– between dependency and autonomy 195-197
patois 23, 180-183
Peirce, C.S. 139-141, 166
performative analysis 163-166
Piot, L.D: 197
pipelet(te) 78, 117-161
place (see also 'belonging and place') 135
private and public (see also 'spying and the public and private') 49-50, 69, 76-77, 90-91, 169-171

R

remoteness 22, 156-158, 171, 184-186
– and event-density 171
resonance 193-194
reversibility of statements 69, 82
Rochet-Lucas, B. 22, 98
Rorty, R. 196-197
Rosaldo, R. 203
rumours 32, 34, 47, 61, 90, 107, 192

S

Sauvages, L'Abbé de 181, 182
Saussure, F. de 139
Segalen, M. & F. Zonabend 12
semiotics 25, 75, 135-143, 167-169, 193
signs (see also 'semiotics,' 'ethnosemiotics,' 'landscape as signs,' 'actions as signs') 10, 24-25, 64, 75, 135-143, 144-145, 188-190
– and frontiers 158
– and identity 188-190
– and intentionality 137-139
– and significance 141-142, 171
– definitions of 137-141
– dimensions of 142-143
– interpretations of 135-143, 144-151, 167-171
– movements as 135, 144, 145-146, 149
– of action 135
– social phenomena as 24
– surfaces as 144, 149-160
– traces as 135, 144, 146-149
silence 9, 32, 49, 51, 63, 73-76, 88-91
– and "culture of silence" 86
– and meaning 74
– and not-hearing 84-85
– and simulating ignorance 86
– "circumstantial silences" 88
– defined 74-75
– "generalized silences" 88-90
– "real silences" 88, 90-91, 165
silence and speech 92
– the paradox of 73, 82, 195
(the) social and the individual (see also 'meaning and the interpreting individual') 26, 193, 195-197, 202
society 25-27
– and discourse 25-27

sorcery, see 'witchcraft'
space (see also 'stories and space') 135, 153
speech, see 'talking' and 'exchange of words'
Sperber, D. 66, 194
spying 10, 136, 160, 167, 169-171, 175
– and the public and private 160, 169-171
– key figures 160-163
Stendahl, H.P. 183
Stocking, G.W. 198
stories 9, 31, 69, 141, 153-154, 169, 175, 191-194, 195
– and morality 45-47, 69
– and myths 61, 65-68
– and space 153-154
– and the social landscape 31
– and the definition of self and others 31, 69
– characters in 45-48
– examples of 36-44
– narrator of 45-46
– paradoxes of 46-47, 195
– telling of 31, 63-64
– themes of 31, 48-62

T

talking (see also 'communication,' 'exchange of words') 9, 63, 73, 75, 141, 169-171, 175, 188-189, 192-194
– about relatives 88
– about talking 75-79
– and social cartography 192-193
– and the power of words 92, 104-108
trop causer 76-78
Turner, V. 119, 163, 165

W

Wikan, U. 194
witchcraft 24, 55-56, 77, 90, 92-107, 113, 123-126
– and being *pris(e)* 95-97, 125
– and healing 125-126
– and jealousy 93-94, 100-103, 131
– and parallel discourse 94, 100, 104, 113, 131
– and sorcerers 93-97, 125-126
– and the annunciator 95-97
– and the bewitched 93-97, 125
– and unwitchers 93-97, 125-126
– as discourse 92-108
– in the Norman Bocage 92-97, 103-104
– rationalization of 103-106